IF IT COULD HAPPEN HERE . . .

If It Could Happen Here . . .

Turning the Small-Membership Church Around

Jeff Patton

Abingdon Press
Nashville

IF IT COULD HAPPEN HERE . . .
TURNING THE SMALL-MEMBERSHIP CHURCH AROUND

Copyright © 2002 by Abingdon Press

This book is printed on acid-free paper

Library of Congress Cataloging-in-Publication Data

Patton, Jeff, 1954–
    If it could happen here : turning the small-membership church around / Jeff Patton.
        p. cm.
    Includes bibliographical references.
    ISBN 0-687-03033-1 (alk. paper)
    1. Small churches—Pennsylvania—Canton (Bradford County: Township)— Case studies. 2. Rural churches—Pennsylvania—Canton (Bradford County : Township)—Case studies. 3. Church growth—Pennsylvania—Canton (Bradford County : Township)—Case studies. 4. East Canton United Methodist Church (Canton, Bradford County, Pa.)
    I. Title.
    BV637.8 .P38 2002
    254'.5—dc21

                                                                        2002000962

02 03 04 05 06 07 08 09 10 11—10 9 8 7 6 5 4 3 2 1

MANUFACTURED IN THE UNITED STATES OF AMERICA

Contents

Foreword

When I first heard the story you are about to read, I believed it only because I knew Jeff Patton and because I believe all things are possible. What you are about to read is real. You can bet the farm on it, take it to the bank, or just take it on faith; but it's real. Jeff will take you on an awesome ride as he shares the lessons learned and the lives changed during the spiritual rebirth of a small, rural church in north-central Pennsylvania. I'm convinced if the miracle of transformation can happen in East Canton, it can happen anywhere. This story needs to be relived a thousand times over.

The U.S. countryside is dotted with thousands of small, rural congregations, most of which are struggling merely to survive. High on their institutional agenda is the collection of enough money to keep a pastor around, to care for the aging members, and to keep the doors of the institution open. Only once in a great while do these congregations connect with the lost, the least, and the suffering. And why should they? After all, they're "just a small church."

Over the past decade and a half, I have had conversations with hundreds of leaders in small, decaying congregations. Those leaders' memories of a faith once lived reveal long and effective congregational heritages. But I detect something else in these conversations. Most of these leaders exhibit signs of "spiritual amnesia." They do not have a clue about why their congregations were started years ago, where the source of their heritages lies, or what they need to do today to be the church of Jesus Christ once again. Most are best described as clubs, museums, or hospices.

Yet within each of these congregations I have stumbled upon a few saints who intuitively know there must be more to faith than what they experience from week to week. And when a spiritual leader like Jeff Patton comes along and fills aching hearts with hope and purpose, these churches explode with new life.

Throughout the book, Jeff will share powerful stories of some of the personal transformations that occurred during the rebirth of East Canton. He does so because this is not a book merely about how to kick start a church from death to life. It's not a book about church growth or church health. It is a book about that which lies at the center of the gospel and every true congregation of faith—transformed lives.

After the first read-through of *If It Could Happen Here . . . ,* I sent the following E-mail to Jeff: "A powerful book." Jeff replied, "What did you find powerful about it?" My response was as brief as my original post: "The stories of personal transformation." Jeff's reply reveals the heart of this man: "That's what it's all about!"

Bill Easum
Mustang Island, Texas
2001

Introduction

Congregations that have experienced long-term declines in membership and attendance are usually seen as difficult projects. Reversing this decline is often referred to as making a "turnaround." Many pastors, congregational leaders, and denominational executives hold out little hope that declining congregations will ever "turnaround." Small rural, declining congregations seem to have less chance of a turnaround. One major factor is that many young people are abandoning rural life for more financially secure urban life. Rural areas in America are seeing an enormous drain of resources and talent.

Almost 70 percent of all churches in America are small, with worship attendance under one hundred.[1] Whether in rural or urban settings, declining congregations face similar obstacles that work against transformation and vitality. Most of these congregations are unable to offer or to sustain life-giving ministries. There simply are not enough resources: not enough people, facilities, people, money, people, or hope. Many of these congregations attempt simply to survive.

In the following pages, you will encounter a congregation that experienced a turnaround and became a lay-led teaching congregation, exporting transforming vitality to neighboring congregations. The lessons learned in this process of "turnaround" are applicable to any congregation that may find itself more concerned with survival than with growth.

In March 1986, I was finishing advanced degree work and considering returning to parish ministry. I specialized in pastoral counseling and received an appealing opportunity. My District Superintendent (DS) asked if I would be willing to take a full-time appointment of two churches in rural north-central Pennsylvania. In addition to the congregations, there was a denominationally related counseling center in a nearby town that had not been staffed for four years. The center's Board of Directors was looking for a pastoral counselor. Serving the counseling clinic would be part of the "full-time" arrangement. I thought, *Wonderful, I could do the counseling I felt called to do and serve these congregations until the counseling clinic could support me full time.* So, with my wife, our new baby, and the hidden agenda that I would serve the church until the clinic took off, I accepted the appointment to the East Canton Charge (East Canton and Windfall Churches), Wellsboro District, Central Pennsylvania Conference of The United Methodist Church.

LEADERSHIP TIP
What are your hidden agendas?

When the DS said "rural," he was on target. It was as Bill Easum called "at the crossroads of nowhere and nowhere."[2] The nearest hospitals and malls were an hour away—one northeast, one north, and one south. At the time, the nearest movie theater was twenty-five miles away. Nevertheless, it was beautiful country with many family farms. The mountains in the fall were majestic. The valley, as some called it, looked like a painting of a New England village with the newly spired East Canton Church standing out as a gem in the crown of mountains. Many families had a deep Yankee heritage. Hardworking and determined, they were the salt of the earth. Like many small towns, East Canton had a cloistered mentality: If your parents' parents were not born there, you were an outsider, even if you had lived there for thirty years. It was not that the people were unfriendly. But, simply put, if you were not related, you were an outsider. So, the first lesson I learned was, do not talk to anyone about anyone else because everyone is related.

LEADERSHIP TIP
Who really teaches you about ministry?

While the valley was beautiful, all was not well there. Family farms were closing each month. Young people were leaving for greater opportunities. Fewer young people wanted to farm for a living, and it was a hard living for those who attempted it. If you did not own your own farm, the expense of buying one was astronomical. There were some factories and service-oriented jobs; but generally, the employment prospects were slim. Divorce rates were high. Children aged 13, 14, and 15 were having babies at an increased rate. Sexual promiscuity and reports of incest abounded. Alcoholism and recreational drug use for both adults and youth were rampant.

Those people were, as Tex Sample describes them, "hard living people."[3] They worked hard, were paid little, and their faces and hands showed it. Some of these people were still milking cows into their eighties because, first, it was something they loved, and second, it was life for them. They tilled the land, planted the crops, and watched and waited each year to see if their efforts would be blessed. They endured good and bad years and increasing costs and lower profits. They were land rich and cash poor (at least some of them).[4] But they were hospitable, welcoming us warmly. These people taught me about hospitality.

The two congregations that comprised the East Canton Charge were East Canton and Windfall. (In 1945, there were five congregations on the circuit.) They were quaint, small, and in need of direction (as well as paint and remodeling). Like most churches, each had a core of dedicated people who had seen many pastors come and go. They had stopped trying to figure out the system. They knew that every four to seven years they would be assigned a new pastor, whether they liked it or not. Their mission was simple—Survive! They attempted to look for the good in each pastor assigned to them, and to their credit they managed to overlook the rough edges in me.

As is also true of many congregations, God had provided a small but dedicated group that had a vague notion that the church was really about reaching other people with God's great love. This group met regularly to pray for the church's many needs and for each other. They understood that God might want to use them to reach their neighbors with hope, love, and a new vision for life. Yet they really did not have a clue as to what they should be or what they should be doing. As we continued to meet regularly for prayer, we asked God to show us what it meant to be the church today, right there in rural Pennsylvania. This was a bold step for the group. They were willing to change. They wanted to make a difference.

And what a difference they made. Everything I thought I knew about ministry was changed, refined, and reworked. It became an adventure to watch each congregation grow, get stretched, grow more, and in the end, become something most said could not happen. Success is more thrilling in situations where others believe there is little possibility for success. This can be your experience, too! The turnaround of a congregation is a wonderful, life-giving experience for everyone involved. While this account of a turnaround congregation is particular to one town, the implications of this turnaround process are applicable, I believe, to declining congregations all across the United States. So please do not limit this experience or hesitate to see your congregation as a likely place for a turnaround.

In the following chapters you will meet real people who were part of this wonderful turnaround. This turnaround changed all we knew and thought about congregational life and health. I have left out most of the negative details because you know them by heart already: those who resist any and all change because they *want power* more than they *love Jesus*. Most resistance to change comes from those who center their negativity on money, control, and the building. Please do not ever allow those who hate change to keep you from your passion. Please do not ever allow those who do not want to grow to convince you that survival is all God has in mind for the declining congregation. Dale Galloway wrote: "It is God's will and purpose that your church should be a growing church and that you personally, along with fellow Christians, should learn how to cooperate with the Holy Spirit in making this a reality."[5]

It is my hope that this account will change how you think about your congregation. If that happens, hold on! You will be on the ride of your life. Because if this kind of a turnaround can happen here, it can happen where you are, too! Who we were and what we experienced is not so very different from who you are and what you can experience. All we did was find six levers that enabled us to turn the congregation around. These levers brought real transformation to this congregation.

LEADERSHIP TIP

Are you cooperating with the Holy Spirit in making your congregation a source of transformational life?

Each lever (prayer, discerning a clear mission, indigenous worship, growth groups, membership that means something, and lay pastoring) helped turn around the congregation. One lever changed our attitude. One changed our understanding of what it means to be the church. One changed our celebrations. One changed how we cared for people. One changed the way we worked. And one made leaders out of disciples. Together, the levers turned around many lives and, in the process, changed the future of this congregation.

So if your church is struggling, attendance is dropping, the building is out of date, programs are boring, or you have people who do not want to change, *but* you know there is more to life in Jesus and you want to experience it, this book is for you.

ONE

Then and Now

I hope that what you are about to read will change you and how you view Christian congregations. This book is about the process of turnaround and how a congregation can overcome many handicaps as it grows into an effective mission-driven, vision-oriented, faith-based, permission-giving community that knows there is more to church life than taking up room in a pew. This can happen where you are!

East Canton was able to overcome many handicaps because of the imbedded heart-driven desire "that all might know Jesus." In addition, this community gradually believed that God really was "able to do immeasurably more than all we ask or imagine" (Eph. 3:20 NIV). We overcame many obstacles because we were willing to care about those who were lost, hurting, and alone. We were able to overcome the handicaps because we understood that new times require new approaches if we are to be effective in reaching people with the good news of Jesus Christ.

Understanding our situation—the times, events, cultural climate, and demographics—was crucial in our success. Until we saw the situation accurately, we continued to operate on faulty assumptions. For example, when we realized how spiritually hungry people were, we addressed their core hungers. Previously we had thought that people simply were not interested in worship. Now we understand that they were interested, but we did not speak their language.

To assist you and your congregation, I will provide an overview of the historical situation of Christian congregations at the beginning of the twenty-first century.

In *The Wizard of Oz*, Dorothy looks around the new world where she has landed and makes the discovery that she's "not in Kansas anymore." When we look at the world around us, we make a similar observation: The world is different, strange, hard to understand, and more complex than ever. Like Dorothy, we can say this is not what we are familiar with. The landscape has changed. Words have new meanings. Humankind is different, more diverse, more intellectually aware, more spiritually open, more resistant to organized religion, and more morally confused.

Our culture, in general, is moving forward technologically, but morally it looks like that of the first-century Roman world. Sure, we have laptops and cell phones in our cars, but ethically, we are in radical decline, declining to the days of Plato when the most clever argument would carry the opinions of the populace. When any action is "okay, as long as it doesn't hurt anyone," it becomes politically incorrect to suggest that there is a God or that our actions have consequences. The philosopher may delight in this condition, the sociologist may have much to research and to detail, the moralist much to bemoan; but like it or not, we are not in Dorothy's Kansas, nor are we in 1959. We are not even in 1999.

Turnaround congregations understand this dramatic shift and changes in culture. Furthermore, they view these changes as opportunities for an invasion of the world with the life-changing message of God's love in Jesus Christ. This is an opportune time for Christian believers, for we face a world that is in moral decline but also wide open to the new life Jesus Christ has to offer. People are more open to spiritual thoughts and ideas now than in the last forty years. Old and new forms of religious expression (both Christian and not) are growing all around us. The search for meaning, in a holistic sense, now captures the attention of many people who appear to have it all but still have no meaning. The opportunity is in front of us. What we do with this opportunity will decide the fate and future of many mainline congregations.

Loren B. Mead details these changes in his work *The Once and Future Church.*[1] According to Mead, the environment the church finds itself in has come full circle from the first century. In the first century, the church was attacked by society. Mission was local, right next door. There was little separation between leaders and followers of the Way. Everyone was in mission and ministry as each person used his or her God-given gifts in service to the cause of Jesus Christ. Then the church entered a period in which it dominated the culture (at least in the West), and in that period, clergy dominated the church. Mission was pushed to the edge of the known world, out of the empire, on to the vast "mission fields" of the unconverted. This Christian era was marked by widespread evangelistic efforts, both pre- and post-Reformation.

LEADERSHIP TIP
Can you see the opportunities in front of you?
What are they?

Mead and others know that this era is over. We have entered what Mead calls the post-Christian period. Bill Easum calls this new era "pre-Christian." In this era, the society is once again hostile to the Christian church. The mission is local once again with only 43 percent of Americans active in a worshiping congregation.[2]

In thriving congregations, clergy no longer dominate. Instead, empowered lay leaders are called to do the lion's share of the ministry. Until recently, the Christian church in America was a major player in the sociopolitical field. Now the church is a noisy minority cast on the sidelines, used and manipulated by the media as extremist or by politicians to get votes. What churches say is no longer trusted. Clergy are not automatically respected. Congregations are viewed with suspicion.

Some churched people wish we could return to the not-too-distant past. Many church leaders, particularly those in the mainline churches of America, built agencies and denominational structures for the sole purpose of keeping the church from changing. Some believe they can hold back the flood of change from the culture and the church by vote and committee. If we just vote against change long enough, perhaps we will return to a time like 1959 when church life was peaceful and people flocked to worship.

What a grand year—1959! A three-story, frame house with garage and large yard and that was close to school cost my parents $8,700. Ike was in, and Kennedy was coming. Change was knocking on the door. A new wind was blowing, and singers were singing against war and telling us "we'd better get out of the way for the times they are a-changin'."[3]

LEADERSHIP TIP
Change happens.
You do not get a vote.
—Merv Thompson

Well, it is not Dorothy's Kansas, and it is not 1959 anymore. The changes have come and are coming, and you and I did not and will not get to vote on them. New times are here, and the post-Christian, postmodern, pre-Christian generations find worship services boring, irrelevant, useless, emotionally flat, or in a word, deadly. These people are moving on. These same generations are more open to spiritual dimensions of life than any generation has been in a long time. What they are not open to is exclusive, narrow, either/or thinking. They also do not have the time to waste on a worship service they do not understand, cannot follow, and that relates little to their lives. Those forms of worship simply do not speak their language. They do not understand what we are doing. Since it does not connect with their hearts, they are not interested in what is offered.

> Everything has changed but our ways of thinking, and if these do not change we drift toward unparalleled catastrophe.
>
> —Albert Einstein

Think for a moment about some of the major changes you have experienced and witnessed in the last twenty years—changes in the roles of men and women, in the way we travel, and how we live. Technology has invaded our homes. We have three computers running in my house most of the time. There are more homes with television than there are homes with indoor plumbing. My cousin's son and his wife just had a baby, and within a few hours of the baby's birth, we saw the pictures. Nothing so special about that except that they live in Japan. The Internet web site they designed for their baby was better than any baby book I've seen. Fresh up-to-the-minute pictures each hour. Technology is changing every part of our lives. We currently heat and cool our home with ground water. That's right, ground water, a geothermal heat pump. No gas, no coal, no wood.

Another area that has experienced rapid change is that of ministry.

Then and Now in Ministry

I often seek out respected pastors who were able to grow congregations to see if they had transformational strategies that enabled them to be effective in their ministries. Stewart was such a pastor in a rural Pennsylvania church beginning in the late 1920s. He was a tall, slightly built man with a broad smile and a fire in his soul and eyes. By comparing Stewart's story with my own, you will have a clearer picture of the drastic differences and changes in pastoral ministry.

I asked Stewart to describe ministry as he experienced it. His story reported most weeks were uneventful. He did sermon preparation and house-to-house visiting, by horse at first and later by car. The congregation bought the car so he could make it to the hospital, some fifty miles away. He officiated many weddings—most without premarital counseling—in the parsonage, at all hours of the day and days of the week. Sometimes he knew they "had" to get married, but that was not very often. He did little counseling in any formal sense. He walked with parents whose children were killed in farming accidents or stood by widows when husbands died of a sudden heart attack. Everyone's children were pretty well behaved, Sunday schools were full, and the church had many families. After World War II, many things changed, mostly for the good—bigger Sunday school classes and many more people in worship. When he retired in 1977, he was tired. He had served the Lord for fifty-seven years, and it was time for him to rest. He continued to be active in pastoral visitation for five years.

What a different story from my experience. In 1977, my first year of ministry in a local congregation, I encountered situations Stewart rarely saw in fifty-seven years of ministry. In my part-time position (twenty hours a week), I spent five to seven hours a week in counseling with youth and adults who were stressed out, inappropriately sexually active, going through parents' divorce, thinking about suicide, and overdosing on drugs, with youth hating their parents and parents at the end of their ropes with their children. Three years later, in my first appointment as a full-time pastor in rural Pennsylvania, as I sat in the parsonage reading, someone knocked on the door. I had been at this new appointment about two months. Standing at my door was a young woman—a daughter of a member of the congregation—who had to talk. She entered the house, sat on the couch, and told me that her father sexually abused her night after night. She had to protect her younger sister whom she knew would be her father's next victim. Divorce and separating couples were common. No one was home anymore. With both parents working, the children had to care for themselves. This was just the beginning.

It is sad that many in today's churches still think that Stewart's days are the norm. How mistaken they are. Seminaries have struggled to keep up. Much of what worked in the late 1950s and early 1960s is irrelevant today. Therefore much of what was being taught in the 1970s and 1980s does not prepare men and women for pastoral ministry in this new postmodern, pre-Christian age. The world around us is lost, seeking spiritual direction; and we think bake sales, rummage sales, turkey suppers, and eighteenth-century ritual will make a difference. There are more people in Wal-Mart or Lowe's on a Sunday morning than in churches. Is that because our services are so exciting? Is that because people just are not interested in spiritual things? I do not think so.

LEADERSHIP TIP
What language does your worship speak?

People stay away from worship because it no longer speaks their language, no longer relates to their needs, and is no longer seen as helpful in their journey through life. If something is not helpful to the journey or life of the individuals in this age, it is very easy for them to sidestep that portion of life and move on to something else that may be more helpful. Again, you may not like this, but you do not get to vote on this change.

Many around us do not know about our Christian traditions or the most basic events in our Christian heritage. The basics of the Christian life are now completely foreign to the vast majority of people.

In 1999, a United Methodist church in Pennsylvania held a regular Friday night dinner for the many people in the city who were homeless or poor. One particular night, the pastor suggested serving the Lord's Supper (Communion) to the people. Holding up the loaf of bread, the pastor said, "This is the body of Christ." As the pastor held up the cup and poured grape juice into the cup, he said, "This is the blood of Christ, which was poured out for you." At that time, many people got up to leave. Those serving the meal intercepted them and asked, "Why are you leaving?" One of the people answered for the group, "We aren't eating anyone's body or drinking anyone's blood." This congregation and pastor made the mistake of thinking that everyone knows and understands what Christians believe. In a pre-Christian world, we must start from the opposite presupposition.

What many pre-Christian people believe about Christianity is that it (and we who follow this Way) are well behind the times. We are viewed as irrelevant, boring, or worse, dangerous. Some portions of this pre-Christian society are openly hostile to the foundational beliefs of the Christian community, especially when our views are contrary to their opinions, preferences, and narcissistic needs and desires.

In a pre-Christian society, we can no longer rely on clergy alone for leadership. Lay believers—those not ordained but gifted by the Spirit—must gain their own sense of leadership and find ways to use their gifts. In a pre-Christian society, the mission of the local congregation is not in some distant land, but usually right next door, around the corner, up the street.

LEADERSHIP TIP
What year are you preparing for? 1959? 1999? 2009?

Consultants working with mainline churches lamentably note that most churches are gearing up for 1959. The leadership of many congregations, now in their sixties and beyond, are looking back, remembering what was and how the "glory days" looked. This nostalgic return, which is quite common for all ages when they begin hitting retirement years, is deadly to the church, which presently finds itself in a society that is openly hostile to its mission and purpose. The resistance to change, coupled with nostalgic longings for the past, stalls the forward progress of the church. In place of authentically transformed lives is showy and powerless religion. Instead of fulfilling the great commission and living the great commandment, congregations specialize in questionable fund-raisers and fight over the color they are going to paint the bathroom or the color of the sanctuary carpeting or who will cook Thanksgiving turkeys for the poor or who will clean the parsonage windows after the pastor gets sick of this and leaves. As congregations resist change, refusing to embrace proven growth principles, they continue to decline in energy, numbers, and options. Instead of lighting a candle in this darkness, congregations (and their leaders) complain about the lack of light. They fight each progressive step of learning the language of this culture that we might speak the timeless truth of God's love to a generation unfamiliar with God and our beliefs.

One form the "resistance to change movement" has taken in our churches is found in the insistence that we use classical music. One percent of the population listens to classical music; yet on Sundays, it is the music of choice. The tempos, keys, and sounds of that style of music are beautiful to the trained ear. They are irrelevant to the vast population of pre-Christian people who live near our houses of worship. Over 80 percent of the U.S. population listen to other kinds of music.[4]

If we are to be effective in the twenty-first century, there are at least five basic changes to American Protestantism that we better understand and prepare to address. If we do not, we will find that the "unparalleled catastrophe" Einstein spoke about will be upon the church. Most churches will not survive it.

First, we no longer live in a Christian world. We are surrounded by those who do not know what we believe, and if they do know, they do not think what we believe makes any difference or sense.

Second, we are in the middle of a technological revolution. The amount of information now available to us is mind numbing. The quantity of information used to double about every fifty years; now information doubles in three years and soon will be down to eighteen months.

Third, we have to understand the death of modernity and the rise of the postmodern mind-set. In the 1950s and 1960s, degrees and credentials were signs of competence; today, that is no longer true. Seminaries, while trying to navigate the minefields of technological and spiritual revolutions, postmodern and pre-Christian mind-sets, and the collapse of Christian worldviews, are increasingly attacked for producing master-level graduates who have trouble relating the gospel to daily living. Many growing congregations are not looking to the seminary for staff. Instead, they hire people who demonstrate competence, no matter what degree they have or do not have. Some of the largest congregations in America are pastored by people who have little or no seminary training.[5]

Fourth, churches are no longer dominated by those who live nearby. The automobile has made driving to church a crucial issue. People who used to be expected to attend the local church now drive in excess of twenty miles to worship at a congregation that has more to offer. Congregations who have vision, room, and parking space will attract more and more people.

Fifth, we need to understand the church is changing its focus. In previous generations, the worship experience of Sunday morning was the focal point for the believing church. This was the time for each believer to receive instruction, hear the Word, sing the songs, and leave with a sense of fulfilling the obligation. At times they left renewed in their personal life of faith. In many growing congregations, this is no longer the case. Sunday morning may meet the needs of the believers who gather, but for many, the entire worship experience is designed to engage the "pre-Christians" and lead them into a new relationship with Jesus Christ as they come to know the love of God in Christ. The explosion of contemporary worship experiences, with fast-paced choruses, quick-moving drama, and frequent use of multimedia[6] is a testimony to the effectiveness of this approach with emerging generations. A "Believers' Service" is often on another night or moved to small (growth or cell) groups that have the basic responsibilities of teaching, discipling, and growing the new (and old) believers in their faith.

Because of these and other changes, we at East Canton began to see a new purpose and sense of mission for our congregation. To live in the present and to seek effectiveness given our culture and the time, we were pushed into making many changes. The following chapters will outline those changes, the rationale, and the results. Throughout this work you will encounter what some have called naive or ridiculous optimism. What you really will find is a deep core value that God really is "able to do immeasurably more than all we ask or imagine." The only problems lie in us, in our willingness to embrace God's mission and God's plan and to do it God's way. Many people told us we never would do what we did.

LEADERSHIP TIP
Who is telling you that your congregation "cannot"?
Why do you believe them?

Is this your experience, too? What worthwhile adventure or project has not been met with a vocal and sometimes forceful opposition? As you think about your situation, how do you wrestle with the conflicting realities of the present situation and the prospects that God really can do more than we can ask or imagine right where you are? It is my hope that after you read these pages, you will find yourself wanting to believe that "immeasurably more than all we ask or imagine" can happen to you.

TWO

"Light for Those in Darkness, Safety for Those in Storms"

In the beginning there was prayer, synergy, and audacity. God brought about this wonderful synchronicity of circumstances and people who dared to dream bigger dreams and to grow beyond all we were told we could possibly be or do. This growth was the direct result of God's intervention with a group of people who took seriously Jesus' word that the mission was to "seek and save the lost." Initially, we understood our mission to be "Light for those in darkness and safety for those in storms" (see Lever 2). This mission was married to a commitment to pray that this group of believers would do what was necessary so that this congregation would fulfill this mission. No dream was too big. No idea was stupid. Anyone willing was essential to the overall mission.

> Now to him who is able to do immeasurably more than all we ask or imagine...be glory in the church. (Eph. 3:20-21 NIV)

Prayer undergirded each step of our journey. The consistent, faithful seeking of God's will and blessing for this project was a crucial cornerstone to the turnaround of this (and any) congregation. People like Terry Teykl of Renewal

Ministries convinced us that first we had to pray.[1] This was the Lord's work. Through a determined commitment to pray for God's will in our midst, we were going to be different. We were going to find what God was doing and get involved in it.[2]

The first changes were slight, hardly noticeable. As we continued praying, our values and beliefs became clearer, and we received a vision for ministry. It became very clear that this boat—our church—was floating without a purpose. We had no idea why we were here. Sure, the Annual Conference worked hard each year to come up with an annual theme or quadrennial goal, but these ideas were often far removed from our experience. We realized we had to begin to dream the dream God had for us. That dream included seven areas of focus:

1. *A mission or purpose statement* that attempted to answer the question, Why are we here? Are we a country club or the church? Shouldn't our mission reflect the teachings of Jesus? Shouldn't we be about the same mission Jesus was about? Shouldn't the "lost" (Jesus' word) matter to us? Who are the lost? Who are we? My challenge was to woo as many of the lost as possible in order to begin owning the mission of the church without losing my patience at how slowly it took some to catch this passion. I wanted to drag them along, as fast as I was being pulled. But I knew that would alienate more than it would capture. Allowing God to be in control of the time line and process and staying actively involved in pushing the congregation toward this goal was difficult for me.

2. *Changing worship patterns.* The eighteenth-century forms of worship were boring and irrelevant to the people around us. If we were going to reach the lost, we needed to be relevant; we would have to learn to speak their language. Hard living people would not be attracted to upscale European forms of worship. We had to make our worship experiences indigenous. My challenge was to

develop and train a team that would be able to speak the language of those around us but not sacrifice the wonder and majesty of the gospel. Helping the team learn this new language was often painstakingly slow.

3. *Laity*[3] had to regain the sense that they *are* the church. The people had to own the process. My postgraduate degree work focused on Ephesians 4:11-12, in which pastors and teachers are to "prepare God's people" for their ministry. For ministry to find its way back into the hands of the people, we needed inclusive, permission-giving teams that were willing to use their God-given gifts for ministry. This could not be a top-down decision. The passion to discover and use one's God-given gifts to accomplish the mission had to germinate and grow from within us as we looked at the needs around us and as we were overtaken by a desire for God's work in this place. Small groups and lay pastoring developed from these teams as we responded to the call and mission God gave us.

My biggest challenge was to retool this congregation for their personal ministry, which was difficult because previous pastors had trained this congregation to believe that their only obligation was to "show up, shut up, and pay up." Some liked that old pattern. Some wanted me to stay the "paid Christian." Others caught the vision, had the desire, were given permission, and excelled using their spiritual gifts.

4. We had to be aware of the *demographics of the area*. Who lived near us? What were they like? What we found scared us. Most of the people around us were in deep trouble spiritually, emotionally, and economically. Marriages were a wreck. Babies were having babies. One year, a tremendously high percentage of the children entering first grade came from single-parent families. These situations reflect real lives falling apart all around us. We were forced to find a way to reach out and care for people around us. My challenge was to empower and equip people to care for those

"not like us." I continually had to help people out of their comfort zones so they might use their gifts to reach out to others. I frequently made people uneasy and uncomfortable.

5. We needed *a new organizational system* that welcomed the new people and that allowed us *to work as a team*. Old forms of governing the congregation were not working. The old "administrative forms of governing a congregation" were designed to keep new people out and to consolidate power in the hands of a few. The smaller the congregation, the more true that statement becomes. Committees hinder and prevent change—it is their job. We had to get beyond committees to a system of permission-giving, servant-empowering ministry teams. My challenge was to free people from the outdated rules and regulations that kept us tied to a mentality that pastors "do" and people "do not."

6. *Membership that means something.* Membership, that is, having your name on the roll, no longer means anything to most people. A simple transfer of letter or a bland confession was not helpful in making disciples. We made membership meaningful by making it a sacrificial giving of oneself as well as an entry point to the road of leadership. My challenge was helping those who already were members to understand that just having your name on a book was not useful or helpful.

7. *A push for excellence.* Mediocrity dominated just about everything the church attempted. The Sunday school lessons were prepared over breakfast on Sunday morning. People often were asked to serve on a committee and then told, "You really do not have to do much." Most everything (from mowing the lawn to singing in worship, from serving on committees to showing up for fellowship meals) was done with only the hope that it would be "suitable" or "good enough." Suitable for whom? was the question. Whose standards, whose ideas? Excellence was in short

supply. So we began a push for excellence in ministry. We attempted to recapture the meaning of "if it is worth doing, it is worth doing well." My challenge was to demonstrate the added benefits of doing "all things well" and to use that message to communicate care to those "pre-Christians" surrounding us.

As we grew and progressed in those areas listed above, we saw immediate results. More and more families began attending weekly worship. Their children began to stretch the capacity of the Sunday school. We were quickly out of room. The problem would not go away. Because East Canton was one of two churches in the charge, starting another service presented a major scheduling problem.[4]

We were attracting many young families with babies and small children, but we had no nursery. So, a Sunday school classroom overlooking the worship hall was turned into a nursery. And more people came. We tore out the front of the church and got rid of the "choir space." We turned the organ and piano around, moved the pulpit back into a small opening in the rear wall, and set up folding chairs. More people came. We had a great problem; we had more people than we could fit in the building. The solution to that problem was not an easy one. We would have to build. What a terrifying thought! There was resistance to building right from the first mention of the word.

At one meeting, a dear saint suggested that we get a video camera, set up chairs in the fellowship hall downstairs (with room for about eighty in this low-ceiling basement area), and show the service down there. That way, "all the new people and their children could worship down there." It really happened. I know you are not surprised. I thought it would be better if we just hung a sign out front that said, "Full! Stay Away!" Why is it that so many church people care more about their own comfort or the building than they do about making room for new people? Why are so many churched people so selfish about their space, their pew, when those outside the church are dying without hope? What is it about the open arms and servant heart of Jesus that we do not understand?

LEADERSHIP TIP
How are you making room for those without hope?

These challenges forced me to confront my own need for turnaround in my thinking and in the day-to-day operation of my life as a pastor. While well trained for the "normal duties" of a Christendom pastor (visiting the sick, caring for the poor, writing sermons, leading Bible studies, refereeing church fights), I no longer was able to conduct business as usual. I could not do it all, no matter how long or how hard I worked. I was being pushed to live out what I believed was the role and gift of a pastor. I would have to change first and consistently stand by my decision to be the pastor God was calling me to be, which did not fit the "job description" of my denominational leaders or of many congregation members.

In this process, I was forced to find my mission and use my passion to allow that mission to control what I did as a pastor. I would have to change worship by sharing alternate styles of worship, helping people who liked traditional-oriented worship to appreciate other nontypical styles of worship. If this turnaround was to happen, I would need an army of people who could do all the work God was calling us to. I had to empower, equip, and mentor others to do everything I was doing. I had to get a better understanding of the people around us and communicate my findings in ways that opened the hearts of the congregations to accept, love, and even like those who "were not like us." This was one of the easiest tasks. Once people began to share Christ's love, it became contagious. I had to free people, including myself, from endless, pointless meetings by enlisting them to serve on mission-oriented teams. I had to help existing members understand the commitment they made when they "joined the church" by helping them understand God's call in their lives. And I was serious about doing "all things well." To accomplish that, it was clear that all of us would have to:

1. do less
2. do those things we were doing to the best of our ability
3. enlist, train, and mentor teams for every aspect of congregational life.

This was both a tremendously freeing time and a tremendously stressful time. As we patiently went forward with this process, we continued to see results that convinced us of the wisdom of these changes and that assured the success of the turnaround.

By 1989, East Canton was out of room. The solution was simple for me: either go full time at the counseling clinic, ask for a new appointment, or commit East Canton to making room for ministry by building the facility needed to do ministry and I would stay. The sanctuary, built in 1832, was now torn apart and only able to hold 120 in worship. There was no room for Sunday school or any other programs. We were growing numerically, but more important, we were growing spiritually. We were beginning to dream new dreams. We were beginning to raise up leaders who were faithful in prayer, hooked by the mission, excited about Christ, open to possibilities, and eager to see what God would do next. While the space issue initially was a problem, gradually it became an opportunity. As people were mentored and teams arose, people began thinking "outside the box." We were serious, wondering if God could really do more and what that would look like for us? Leaders in the congregation who were praying and sharing together began to sense God's movement in our midst. Anything was possible.

For me, the central issue was simple: build or leave. I wondered if the leaders had the faith to trust God in this turnaround and if these leaders could be encouraged to step out of their old ways and see a new way. We were at a crossroads. Either we made room, or it was time for me to leave. I began praying earnestly about this with my wife and others. One Monday night during a small-group meeting, someone made the comment that God really wants us to know what to do. Our problem is we do not trust God enough to listen, and when we do listen, we are not sure it is from God. At the close of that study, as we were praying, I wrote down a sentence that came to me. Was it God? Or was the pepperoni on the pizza bad? I did not know. I needed a clearer answer. I may have just received my answer, but like most of us, I was not sure it really was God. Does God use our intuitions? Not many of us can say we have ever heard God, at least not audibly heard God. Yet many people say they have known God was speaking to them in various ways, with various signs, symbols, sounds, and in their thoughts and intuitions. So often when I am quiet before God with a pressing issue, I never hear much that I can rely on. I often hear what I want to hear. In this case, if I did have a preference, it was to fulfill the hidden agenda I started this process with; that is, to make the counseling clinic the full-time job. But I was willing to stay if turning this congregation around was possible. When the sentence came to me that night, I was aware it felt like more than just my own head. In the quiet expectation of the hour, it felt like God was saying something to me. Like Gideon, I needed confirmation.

Debbie, one of the small-group leaders at East Canton, was awakened in the middle of that night by the light of the lamp beside her bed. After asking her husband why the light was on (he had no clue), she turned the light out. In the quiet of the night, she began praying, wondering why the light had come on. Very clearly she heard a message she was to tell me as soon as possible. The message was "stay and build and I will pour down the blessing so much that the walls will not contain it." The next morning Debbie made an appointment to see me. Oddly enough, those were the same words I had written in my journal at the small-group meeting the night before. What she told me compelled me to put my hand to the plow and not to "look back." Many times in the middle of the struggles (like when we asked the wrong person to fill a position, when a dissenting faction decided we should choose to stay small, or after someone told me I had ruined their church), I remembered the word of God to a small-group leader. Coincidence? Hardly. God? Likely!

We stayed, pushed ahead with growth, and watched as God did one wonderful thing after another.

East Canton, against the advice of some at the Annual Conference, planned, financed, and built their new building in 1993. The majority of the work for the $450,000-plus renovation and building project was done with volunteer labor in a three-week-long "work camp" (without the volunteer labor, the price tag would have been double). The building was ready by December 1993 and was paid off in 1996. This congregation of 118 members (140-plus average for worship at that time) accomplished what many thought was impossible. Through those years, we further developed lay-empowered teams to do almost everything. Even the Building Team was operated in this manner, and I only attended two or three meetings of the Building Team in the three years of the process.

In this process, core leaders began to arise in our midst. These leaders became the driving force of the turnaround in the congregation as they passionately gave themselves to the mission and vision God had placed in their hearts. These core leaders of all ages were trusted by the congregation and were known for their integrity and their willingness to live transparent lives for Jesus Christ. You will meet some of them later in the book. Because of their passion and love for Christ, many of the challenges we faced were met in extraordinary and wonderful ways.

In 1993, these core leaders deconstructed most of the other committees and formed one team called the Envisioning Team. The Envisioning Team had two main responsibilities, or subteams called "circles," Empowerment and Outreach. At the Envisioning Team meetings, we did not read the treasurer's report, we did not have votes (ever!), and we rotated the leadership each month. This team began to dream great dreams for the work of God in the area. Prayerful discernment was the major decision force for the team's work. Ideas were put forth for everyone to pray about. As people were led by God, many wonderful tools were developed, which we would have never imagined if on our own. You could never vote no; instead, you could pray that God would help us fine-tune every idea before we attempted it. Even the way we raised money changed. We began to have stewardship emphasis, stressing the joy of tithing. We asked members to estimate what their tithe would be, and based on those figures, the finance team constructed a proposed budget. We understood that there would be other expenses throughout the year that no one had counted on. We also understood that money was never the issue (see Lever 5).

The Envisioning Team developed programs to attract new people, like "Karate for Christ" and "Line Dancing." The Envisioning Team held public forums before state elections and served great desserts. We held free car washes. We organized mission trips to hurricane-stricken zones like Charleston, South Carolina. We hosted Wild Game Dinners, serving bear, elk, and deer. At each event the mission statement governed the activity. At each event the good news of God's love was *light for those in darkness and safety for those in storms*. We even turned our successful fund-raiser (apple dumplings) into mission support. We decided to give every penny of profit from our fund-raisers to missions and to trust God for money. We never missed the money. God always supplied our every need.

In 1994, the core leaders developed a Lay Pastors' school that trained leaders to take more responsibility for ministry and mentoring. And we continued to develop small groups. At one time, over ten small groups (not counting Sunday school and youth groups) met each week.

And we continued to grow.

In 1995, the core leaders developed a teaching church model to export our success to other congregations. *Preparing God's People* was a tremendous success. We would open our homes to pastors and their leadership teams, allowing them to see what a turnaround rural church could do and how they could do this where they were.

In 1996, East Canton and Windfall decided to become independent from each other. By June 1997 each congregation had purchased its own parsonage and planned to welcome a new pastor to their team-based ministry model.

While the big story at East Canton was the turnaround, all the changes must be considered. That turnaround included the permission-giving teams, small groups, the empowering and equipping of people for their ministry, the blended and contemporary worship, lay pastoring, peer counseling, the new building, and outreach programs. Underneath the church's turnaround were the lives that were transformed because of a direct encounter with Jesus Christ. Both the church and its congregation were transformed. What is more important? I cannot say. I only know that as the turnaround process was embraced, lives were changed within the congregation and, as a result, outside the congregation as well. Jesus made a difference in the daily living of so many ordinary lives in the church, and those lives began to touch others.

LEADERSHIP TIP

If turnaround produces changed lives,
what reason is there to resist turning your
congregation around?

As a congregation discovers its mission, purpose, its reason for being, and comes alive, the power of God flows like a river in its midst. This life-changing river of influence begins to change the world it touches. This is not unusual. This is what it means to be the church. Lives are changed. People are affected, changed, transformed, and at times brought back from death—people like Duane.

Duane

It was the third time Duane was arrested for drunk driving, and he was going to jail for ninety days. Duane was never in church much. It was too boring and filled with people who thought they were better than they were. But now his life was in trouble. His wife, Lori, had been attending a small group that met weekly in East Canton. She had been in worship a few times when his arrest and conviction hit their lives like a tornado.

Duane had been in trouble before—tickets, rehab, drug and alcohol problems. Now he was on his way to jail. Life was crashing down, and he had nowhere to turn. The family was tired of his failures; his wife was concerned he would never be any different. And his being in jail was embarrassing for his three children.

So with nothing to lose, Duane and his wife made an appointment to see me. In my office, he told me his life story and asked what is the meaning of life. We immediately began talking about Jesus and if they knew Jesus. They knew about Jesus, but they did not know Jesus. I asked if they would be willing to meet Jesus. His wife said she had committed her life to Christ years ago but had not stayed close over the years. Duane would have to think about it. His situation was killing him, and he was making a mess of everything and wanted to change. When they left my office, I asked them to talk to God about their situation, to talk to God just the way we talked to each other. Ask God to make this clearer.

By the next meeting, Lori had prayed with the members of her small group to rededicate her life, asking Jesus to take charge of her life. Duane was not sure. He did not want to be religious, and he did not want to be a hypocrite. Who does? He did not want to use this crisis in the hope that God would let him off. I did not think God or the state would let him off. But I pressed him anyhow: Would he be willing to ask Jesus to make him different and to make it obvious to him? He said yes. We prayed.

The next week, a new man came into my office. He was ready for jail, ready to be what he should be, ready to allow God to lead him. Duane had attended an AA meeting, gotten a sponsor, and was ready to break the deadly cycle of addiction. Sure, he was frightened of jail. Sure, he was embarrassed. His children's pain was almost too much for him. He still carries the memories of looking into their eyes as he left for jail.

I went with Duane to the courthouse and escorted him to jail. I regularly visited Duane in jail. Ninety days later, Duane went home.

Now, years later, Duane leads the contemporary service and the youth at East Canton. He continues to direct the AA for youth at the church. His children are the leaders of the Christian fellowship at the local school.

Duane called me recently to say that he got his five-year sobriety coin, but even more important, that three youth came to Christ last week. He recently bought a bus and now picks up youth all across the area. They had forty in their youth meeting last week, and they are still growing. Now Duane believes God is calling him to do more, perhaps leaving a very successful carpentry career and raising livestock to enter youth ministry full time. Scary but exciting.

So you see, the excitement at East Canton was not the changes in format, not the blended worship, not the permission-giving teams, not even the new building. What was exciting was seeing the changed lives of the people who found new ways to experience the reality of Jesus Christ in their hard living, daily lives!

THREE

The End of "Pastor Fetch" and the Beginning of "People Go"

The first year in a pastoral appointment (new church) is usually the time to meet everyone. That means people arrive at the door of the parsonage soon after your arrival. Sometimes they are there before you arrive. Usually there are one or two people who have a servant's heart and who genuinely want to know what they can do for you. These people want you to succeed. They have a vested interest in the success of the congregation. They are kind, giving, and willing to open their homes and their hearts to you.

During the first week, many others drop by. Some want to see if you can be recruited for their pet project. Some want to see what kind of pastor has come to their community. Some want to let you know they have the power and if you want to do well you will ask for their opinion and follow it. Bill Easum calls these people "super Max and super Maxine."[1] As time goes by, you will sense their pressure and recognize that they operate with an "us or them" mentality. Those not for us are against us, is usually how this works. It has been my experience that the most faithful servants and the most unchanging control fanatics find their way to the parsonage door in that first week. It often takes time to discover who is really whom.

LEADERSHIP TIP
Who controls your time?

Those interested in control usually have an agenda that requires the pastor's obedience or alienation. Often the agenda has to do with the addictions common in congregations.[2] Those addictions center on children, youth, the building, and money or more commonly referred to as "the four thousand reasons why we cannot spend one penny of the endowments unless it is designated, and we only designate endowments for the building." If you read that last quote again, start with a soft voice and end by yelling the last phrase, and you'll get the idea. I have found that those with control issues are usually concentrated in one of two places, although you may find them in other places as well. The places I usually run into trouble with people are in the trustees and in the choir. Bless the pastors who have both areas filled with "Controlites."[3]

Pastor Fetch

Regardless of where your controlling people are centralized, they usually have one major goal: to train each pastor to be their personal chaplain—what others call "pastor fetch." Personal chaplains once were common in Europe. Each family would pay for their own priest who would care for the souls of the family. Pastors, in an attempt to gain personal satisfaction or maybe because there was nothing else to do, often allowed themselves to become personal chaplains, serving the needs of people who paid them. I still find people, even in large churches, who believe they pay their pastor to "care for them." Recently I was talking to a youth director who had met with local pastors. The youth director was thinking about strategies to reach the many pre-Christian youth in the area. One of the pastors present debated the wisdom of those ideas: "We must take care of the youth in our church first."

LEADERSHIP TIP
Those "not here" are just as important as those here!

I do not believe we are to spend the majority of our time "caring for each other." *We are to go and make disciples.* Those who adopt the personal chaplain mentality usually are convinced that as their congregation declines they must spend more and more time caring for the few remaining chosen (and sometimes frozen) participants. Thus the downward spiral accelerates and the congregation declines even more.

This attitude of "care-taking" is pervasive in our congregations. In order to make sure pastors stay personal chaplains, congregations have to train each pastor. When I arrived at East Canton, I met with wonderful people eager to see the new guy and to discern if I had been trained in this game of "pastor fetch." The previous pastors had spent a majority of their time visiting in homes, attending dinners, going to the hospitals, and holding the hands of all the sick, ill, and otherwise shut in and discontented. When the bone was thrown, the pastors abandoned families, days off, and holidays, and ran to fetch the bone, thus proving their worth and making all the Controlites happy.

Is This Your Story?

In 1986, East Canton had 227 names on the role, and only 55 people regularly attended worship. There were many people to meet and visit. And each of them had someone else who desperately needed a visit. "Pastor, could you please find some time to visit Mary? Mary is my third cousin's mother's sister's daughter. She has a teenage daughter; well she is twenty-two now and has this baby. I know if you visit them they will really appreciate it. Thanks." The willingness to play "pastor fetch" is fed directly to pastors by many books of "pastoral care" and denominational rule books of pastoral behavior, which imply "good pastors" visit regularly in homes. I still hear denominational officials insisting that pastors are to "be in each home each year." Add to this demand the need to be needed, and I know of pastors who cannot say no. You throw the bone; they will fetch like a young puppy that cannot wait to run after the bone one more time. What a terrible waste of time and misuse of the pastoral office.

LEADERSHIP TIP
What about your weekly routine
looks more like pastor fetch than
empowers others for their ministry?

Visiting people who did not want anything to do with Jesus unless it had to do with hatching (birth or baptism), matching (weddings), or dispatching (funerals) was annoying, time consuming, and from what I saw in many of my colleagues, pointlessly exhausting. On the rare occasion that I would visit one of these people, often they would not even turn the television off. I developed a different approach to the care of the congregation.

That different approach for visiting (see Lever 6) was to train others with appropriate gifts (compassion, mercy, faith, and others) to undertake the visitation of people in the congregation. As part of my understanding of pastoring, I empowered, equipped, and mentored others to visit with people who were ill, shut in, or otherwise unable to attend worship. I simply could not and would not attempt to do everything. By training others, many more people were freed to do the necessary visiting in the congregation. I simply was unwilling to sacrifice my family at the altar of "pastor fetch." If you needed to speak to the pastor, you were asked to make an appointment to see me in the office at an available hour. We took the phone off the hook for meals and family time, and days off were days away.

This does not mean I did not visit at all. If life situations were severe, such as a death, I would go. I spent the majority of my time visiting in prisons and with people who were searching for life. I modeled what I thought all Christians should do, that is, to seek out the lost and help them find the love of God in Jesus. I also spent time with the congregational leaders. I often visited in the homes of those who were leading small groups. I routinely stopped by to meet with the small-group leaders (see Lever 4) and the lay pastors (see Lever 6).

This practice made many longtime members very unhappy with me. When they had their gallbladders removed or ingrown toenails operated on and I did not visit, they would moan and groan. Usually they were home in two days anyway. Many of those who were unhappy thought I was paid for this kind of hands-on "personal chaplain" fetch. I was the "paid Christian" after all. Unfortunately for them I never felt that call in my life. I never wanted to be the "paid Christian." I did everything I could to break the crusty, old, dysfunctional habits, in which the pastor did it all and the people did little or nothing.

The Eternal Childhood of the Believer

The role, or more properly the gift, of pastor is to equip believers for their ministry, not do the ministry (Eph. 4).

Pastors are to empower, equip, and train God's people for *their* ministry. The gift of pastor is an equipping gift. Pastors are not to "do all the ministry." It simply is not in the Scripture. Furthermore, this attitude contributes to a condition I see in most congregations. This condition is called "the eternal childhood of the believer."[4]

Why is it that in almost every Protestant congregation there are people who have been in the church most of their lives and who would not know the first thing about leading another person into a personal relationship with God through Jesus Christ? What would you say to someone who asked you about the life you have in Christ? If they wanted to have that life in their lives, what would you tell them? Go see the pastor? Since so many "church members" do not know the basics about Christian evangelism, they tend to spend vast amounts of time in unproductive, mission-less activities, which are "religious" but disconnected from any type of transformational ministry. Consequently we have congregations full of people who have had an encounter with Jesus Christ but who have never matured, staying a child for eternity.

Some symptoms of the eternal childhood of the believer are:

- never leading anyone to Christ.

- fussing and complaining when they do not get their way, and even threatening to take their money and run if things are done that they dislike.

- paying the pastor or staff to be the "Christians" and thereby freeing themselves from any obligations to live the Christian life (and sadly miss the joy of the Christian life as well).

Because they are so concerned with what is in it for them, social justice, evangelism, and mercy ministries never get off the ground. After all, "how will this benefit me?"

The Beginning of "People Go"

It is my conviction that the sole or main role of the pastor in the worshiping community of the twenty-first century is to nurture or equip the believers in Christ *for their ministry.* At a recent presentation, Bill Easum presented a slide that stated that in the twenty-first century, "pastors will no longer... teach, preach, counsel, visit, sit on committees, administrate, lead worship, or any other task usually associated with pastoring."[5] The sighs were heavy, and the gasps were loud. One pastor asked, "What will we do?" Bill answered, "You will prepare and train others to do all of those tasks."

What were the sighs and moans all about? Pastors have been trained to think that "ministry" is their job. That means every ministry a congregation attempts ought to have the "professional" in control, whether it be teaching confirmation class or leading the adult Bible study or visiting in the nursing home or _____ (fill in the blank). If it is "ministry," the "minister" ought to do it. Thus when confronted with this new understanding of ministry as the work of all the people of God, pastors often wonder what will be left for them to do if the people of God do the "ministry." The notion that only the "ordained" can baptize, offer Communion, teach confirmation, lead Bible studies, run the worship service, preach, and counsel is not only unbiblical, but also ineffective. It furthers the false notion that clergy "do" and laity "do not."

As in baseball or any other team sport, being relegated to the sidelines or sitting on the bench leads to apathy and boredom. If I cannot play, have no hope of ever getting in the game, why bother to sit on the bench? But if I can be part of the team, using my gifts to help the team be its best, then I come to the game each day with excitement and anticipation. I find ministry to be equally exciting when I can participate.

While first-century pastors equipped and empowered believers to live for God, Christian congregations of the last fifty years feature clergy who attempt to do it all, who burn out quickly and painfully, and who usually take their families down with them. How can you expect a person to carry the collective weight of any given congregation? How can one person ever think he or she could, let alone should, attempt to be the "minister"? No wonder so few men and women stay in ministry for the long term. The tasks of ministry are more than one person—or even a staff—can possibly accomplish while maintaining emotional, physical, and spiritual health.

The people of God suffer too as valuable gifts go unused, as gifted people sit on the pews with no hopes of ever being asked to use their gifts. Some get used to it. Others go where they can use their gifts and be a part of the team, playing in the game.

As the East Canton congregation became aware that I would not play "pastor fetch," that instead I was eager to grow the church, they stopped telling me about their mother-in-law's third cousin's brother's second wife. Instead, when they told me about someone who needed a visit, I would usually ask, "Have you been there first?" They usually would shake their head no. I then would say, "You go, and if the situation is more than you can handle, next time I will go with you." I also began training people to be lay pastors (see Lever 6), and soon these people began visiting others as well. Within a short time, I had more and more people who were willing to use their gifts for God.

The preparation, study, and reading I had to do to prepare people for their ministries was extensive. By allowing others to use their gifts I never ran out of things to do. We had small groups, lay pastors, peer counselors, bereavement groups, AA groups, spiritual enrichment weekends, youth groups, children's programs, and food programs. Each area took time to mentor, train, and guide leaders.

Just so you do not get the wrong impression, you need to know that some people never stopped attempting to get me to play "fetch." They could not get it through their heads that I was not interested. And some were just angry and wanted to see what it would take to get me to visit. At each quarterly Pastor Parish Relations Committee meeting for the first three or four years I knew I would hear about not visiting. Someone was upset and hurt that I "did not like them enough" to visit.

Today, I advocate an even more intense policy. If I visit someone, I insist that someone go with me, that I might mentor that person to use his or her gifts in visitation with the sick and needy. The day of clergy-dominated congregations is just about over. The day of lay empowerment is here. Postmodern people will not be content to remain spectators. They want to be participants at the center of the action. Therefore pastors must mentor or coach the congregations to be all they can be, allowing them to use their gifts for the sake of the kingdom. As congregations reach more people it is essential to have more people trained to use their gifts.

FOUR

Lever 1: Prayer

They devoted themselves to the apostles' teaching and to the fellowship, to the breaking of bread and to prayer.

(Acts 2:42 NIV)

Prayer is a mysterious thing. Many of the greatest movements in the church began with prayer. Prayer is central to the work of God and is essentially linked to the movement of the Holy Spirit in a person's life and to the community of faith. Of course many say that prayer is nothing more than wish fulfillment or at best a contemplative effort to dive more fully into the depths of one's soul.

Many Christians hold that prayer is much more. Prayer is foundational to a relationship with God. Prayer is not just a one-way monologue, but an active dialogue with the "God who is there and who is not silent."[1] Prayer is essential to the life and health of each believer and therefore essential to the life of each congregation. Unfortunately few believers spend much time in prayer. Ten minutes a day is often considered a lot of time, and the thought of spending hours in prayer is almost unheard of outside the walls of the monastery.

When I arrived at East Canton, there were six or seven people who met each Wednesday at 7:00 P.M. for one hour of prayer. This was not a time for the weak hearts or lazy followers. This was a time of earnestly wrestling with the mysterious issues of life and death, God's will, and our own desires and hindrances to our faithfulness. This was a time of seeking God's will for our individual lives and the life of the congregation. The prayers were sincere and at times painful. By the time I left East Canton eleven years later, there were people praying at many times and in many places. People met for prayer on Sunday morning, Monday evening, Wednesday morning, Wednesday evening, Thursday night, and Saturday morning. Prayer became an important aspect in the personal devotional life of this congregation. This emphasis on prayer had an impact on every area of congregational life.

We decided that prayer was so important we would dedicate a room in the new building for prayer. This room was open and available for prayer seven days a week. We placed a white board in the room and listed the "top ten" prayer concerns for the congregation. When you entered the room, which was furnished with a nice couch and chairs, you would see the white board and immediately know what to pray for while there. There were pamphlets on prayer and lists of prayer concerns in the room. This room was regularly used by members and attendees of East Canton as well as by people from other congregations.

East Canton had periods of prayer emphasis when we would ask people to pray and even to fast (i.e., give up eating for a period of time that we might pray). We would pray for people, for health, for missionaries, for mission projects, and for discernment as we attempted to know and do God's will. More people began to take seriously the call to prayer and people did in fact pray more. Not only did more people pray but also studied and read about prayer, which in turn produced a desire in many to pray more. Again, the Sunday morning message was an opportunity to teach and experiment with prayer. A sermon series covered practical aspects of prayer, such as how to give up the shopping list of requests and instead to seek God, how to spend time listening as well as talking to God, and how to focus prayers on others instead of ourselves.

We encouraged all attendees to spend ten to twenty minutes each day in prayer. Usually we were told they could not do that, that they were too busy, or that they could not concentrate that long. We challenged them to try. In a few weeks, they would return with stories of how wonderful their time with God had become, now that they were listening for God and focusing on others instead of on themselves.

During the planning and construction of the new building, prayer was crucial and essential to the growth and success of the project. I do not have time to tell you how God repeatedly intervened and brought together key elements of the project. I hope one incident will suffice.

The East Canton congregation needed to make room for ministry. After much prayerful discernment, the congregation decided to renovate the existing sanctuary and add a 50-foot by 70-foot three-story addition. To accomplish this, we hosted a "volunteer work camp." This work camp enlisted people from across Pennsylvania and the northeast who would give labor skills in exchange for room, board, and a great time with other Christians.

In the design of the building aspects such as design features, ministry needs, and space issues were prayerfully discerned. The design of the front entrance to the worship center was one concern. There was a large space above the main doors. As we prayed, people sensed (what else would you call this) that there should be a stained-glass window in that space. This was added to the prayer list, but with all the more "important" details of housing and feeding over three hundred people, open window space was soon forgotten. During the second week of the volunteer work camp, two women (one from Massachusetts, one from New Hampshire) were standing in the hall, looking at that space above the entrance door. Both of these women, who had met for the first time that morning over coffee, were talking to one of the women from East Canton who was on the building team. The woman from Massachusetts asked what was to be in that space. The woman from East Canton told them of the desire for a stained-glass window. Both women gasped and looked at each other. The first woman said, "I wondered why I felt I should be here. Now I know. I design stained glass for a living." The other woman said, "I, too, wondered why I was coming here. I'm not a carpenter or good with hammers. I build stained-glass windows for a living." The woman from East Canton dropped her jaw and was amazed for the thousandth time at how God had prepared each aspect of the building. If you go to East Canton, look at the window as you enter the sanctuary. The glass sunrise matches the wooden one carpenters carved in the front of the church in 1832. The grapes and wheat are traditional Christian symbols. The window is a beautiful testimony to God's hand, even in the little things. I believe all of this was the direct result of so many people praying for each and every aspect of the facility. I could go on for hours about the prayers that were answered in the building process alone.

Prayer is a mystery to most of us. We believe in God, we know that Jesus prayed, and yet most "church people" spend less than two minutes a day in prayer. Why?

Sure, people pray for life but still die. The East Canton congregation watched one of our strongest pray-ers suffer and die. It was hard to know why there was not a physical healing; the many people she prayed for knew that her healing came through death. Isn't it strange that after this strong praying person died, many more people began to pray?

I cannot explain it and would not want to try, but I know that God is able to do so much more with us when we honestly seek God in prayer. Prayer changes us. Prayer is a vital pathway of transformation as we live out our faith in a real world.

I also know that many of the people who tended to be against everything new were not people of prayer. Often these people confronted me with why something would not work or was wrong to attempt. I said to them, "Please pray about this, and if you can say that you know for sure that God is not in this project, please let us know. For we have been praying and we are open to hear from God. So please pray." No one ever came back with "fresh news" about God's disfavor of our plans. I would have loved to hear that they were praying, but many of those who complained the most prayed the least. (The same is true about money. Generally those that fuss the most give the least, and those who give the most fuss the least.)

Prayer is mysterious. We cannot control it, we cannot demand our own way, we cannot rub the "Buddha," click our heals together, and expect to get our own way. Prayer is transformational; that is, when we encounter God in prayer, *God changes us*. We become different when we pray.

At East Canton, we found prayer was a lever that promoted our growth and encouraged our development both as individuals and as a congregation. This simple but overlooked reality is that without a foundation of prayer, little is accomplished. Without a dedicated core group of people who were willing to spend time with God in prayer, East Canton's spiritual health would have suffered greatly.

One key element in that success was the amount of prayer dedicated to the protection and guidance of the leadership, including me and my family. Terry Teykl's book, *Your Pastor: Preyed On or Prayed For*,[2] details the importance and crucial aspects of undergirding your leadership with prayer. It is Terry's conviction and my experience that pastors who do not have a dedicated group praying for them are never as effective as those pastors who have such prayer support. The spiritual warfare mentioned in Ephesians is rampant in the churches that are growing and effective. Every emphasis or opportunity for growth is challenged and attacked. Some of that resistance comes from spiritual powers. Without prayer, the congregation and its leadership are weaponless to defend themselves against the spiritual attacks that will come to that community.

LEADERSHIP TIP
If you are a pastor are you "preyed on or prayed for"?
—Terry Teykl

How many pastors and leaders of growing congregations have you witnessed fall apart, ruin their lives, commit stupid acts of immorality, and end the transformational move of the Holy Spirit in their midst? I have seen this time and time again. Do not tell me there is not a war going on, for I have been to the trenches and seen the wounded, heard the cries of the dying, and seen the results of war when the church has neglected its chief weapon—prayer—against the war. How many pastors burn out each year because there was no one praying for them? How many congregations barbecue and fry their pastors without ever taking the time to pray for them? How many pastors return home after a Sunday worship and fall asleep, exhausted from the fight with one more person who wants a piece of their hide? Many pastors wonder what it would be like to have a congregation that spent more time in prayer than in complaining. Let me tell you what it was like.

I knew that there were people—lots of people—who were praying for me and my family every day. These people were there when life turned bad, when parents died, when children were injured, and when I was ill. These people regularly were before God with my name and the names of those in the congregation who were hurting on their lips. Maybe it is all coincidence, or maybe the wonderful years of growth were the result of these people taking seriously the call to pray. I can never give coincidence the credit for the hand of God in the lives and growth of the East Canton church. Prayer was frequent, fervent, and, as a result, effective. God moved, and we were blessed to be a part of God's hand in our midst.

To attempt to grow a congregation without this lever is to cause the whole project to collapse. Prayer is a crucial lever, and I would say the central lever that turns the entire process while simultaneously holding all things together.

Because of the seriousness of the need for prayer, we always looked for ways to make prayer more real, more meaningful, and more consistent in our lives.

FIVE

Lever 2: Discerning a Clear Mission

One of the first tasks at East Canton was to help the congregation consider its purpose by discerning its mission, its reason for being, its passion. We thought that if any congregation is to be effective, it must be able to answer the question "why are we here?" That is the purpose of a mission—a deep-seated, passionate discerning of purpose.

Many congregations have no idea what their purpose or mission is. Congregations drift year in and year out with no idea of what God is doing and with only vague ideas of what it means to be the Body of Christ. Congregations have vague notions of "loving one another" while the business of weekly services, choirs, rehearsals, meetings, and crises occupies most hours from Sunday to Sunday. In my experience, even congregations with purpose or mission statements do not know what the statement contains and consequently have no vision or mission.

My first talk (sermon) at East Canton in July 1986 was from Proverbs: "without a vision, the people perish." What was the compelling vision of this congregation? How was it that a building erected in 1832 still had ample room in 1986? For the next several weeks, I reflected and communicated my observations that while East Canton was outwardly religious (that is, we had services, a building, and committees), we were inwardly void of meaning and disconnected from the God of the New Testament, with most constituents having no idea why this congregation was here.

For me, the vision was the first and most crucial aspect of congregational life. With no vision, the people would perish. If we do not have a vision for God's work in this place, how can we survive let alone thrive? And if the vision was not a passionate longing for God to be real in our midst, I knew there would not be many changed lives. Furthermore, the purpose of the church—to make disciples—would not be accomplished without a vision and a mission. I began pushing people to get in touch with God's passion for this place.

At first I thought coming up with a mission would be easy. We could state the purpose of the church in one sentence and be done. We would have a unifying mission statement that would be the center point for all we are and do. In 1986 and 1987, as we gathered the Administrative Council to discuss these ideas, it became clear this was going to be a long educative process with many bumps along the way. People had very different ideas about the purpose of the church. I began a sermon series on the need for vision and what an appropriate mission might look like for a congregation in a secular, superstitious, pre-Christian world filled with many competing "spiritual" ideas. A clear vision is essential in the formulation and ownership of a dynamic, life-giving mission statement.

In that series, I de-emphasized maintaining the building and stressed the need for each person to be in ministry. What is our purpose? Why were we here? What was God calling us to do? What were we going to do with the gifts God has given us? And how was God going to use us to make a difference in our world, right here, right now?

LEADERSHIP TIP
"Tell me your vision and I will tell you your future."
—Dale Galloway (20/20 Vision, p. 13.)

Next, I turned our focus from looking at ourselves to looking at the community. We explored the demographics and psychographics of the area. We purchased a demographic study by Percept.[1] We took a hard look at the area five and ten miles from the building. What we saw scared us: drugs, an extremely high teen pregnancy rate, alcohol addiction, failed marriages, abandoned children, and worse—irrelevant churches still viewing bake sales and suppers as their major evangelistic tools. How could we reach out to the people around us who were hurting and literally and spiritually dying? How could we learn that Jesus was more interested in those outside of our walls than he was in bake sales, committee meetings, and irrelevant eighteenth-century worship? Could we risk leaving the comfort of knowing everyone and reaching out to those who are not like us? These were hard questions that demanded more than casual answers.

The first mission statement took almost two years to construct. The main input for this statement came from me and from the group that met for prayer each week. It was in the prayerful discernment of our purpose that the vision and the words of the mission statement became life for us.

Of course we had those who resisted change. We heard the seven last words of a dying church ("We never did it that way before") so many times we began joking about it. Those who were used to being in control had a difficult time with a God who would not stop the growth and with a pastor who did not care about what was, but always talked about what could be. With a clear mission, now adopted by the Administrative Council, we finally had a direction, a reason for being. We also had a lens by which we could focus all our efforts.

Finally a Clear Vision

After the two-year process of refining the mission statement and praying, we believed we had a major role to play in the plan of God for this community. Our vision was to touch lives so they might know Jesus. Our mission was to reach out to those around us with God's love. In 1989, the Administrative Council constructed and adopted a mission statement that would answer the question "why are we here?" It read:

> *To nurture believers in Jesus Christ and*
> *To be light for those in darkness*
> *And safety for those in storms.*

We chose the word "nurture" to indicate our desire for each person to be all he or she can be for God by using his or her gifts and serving God in daily life. At East Canton, nurturing believers meant helping the already committed understand what it means to live connected to Jesus Christ. Nurturing meant understanding the vision and mission of the church and doing all you can to reach that vision. Nurturing meant preparing the already committed to be leaders in this congregation. Nurturing believers meant teaching each believer that our primary purpose in life is to reflect the love of Jesus Christ in everything we do. It meant teaching each believer to host and to run small groups. It meant learning about spiritual gifts and using the gifts God has given you. It no longer meant just filling a pew, but becoming a lifelong learner and a disciple of Jesus.

> The church is not a club for the comfortable but a saving station for the world.
> —Bishop Felton May
> (Annual Conference Message, 1990)

After examining our world, we realized that many people were living in a terrible darkness. They had little hope and were addicted to substances that ruined their lives and made them unable to hold down good jobs. This pre-Christian culture had lost its hold on the values of life and was now wandering in the dark, unsure of which direction to travel. These people were hungry for life and meaning.

Another group of people had lived and suffered in the darkness. Abuse was rampant, incest was high, children were frightened, and women were battered and scarred. Just being light would not be enough. We had to be more than light; we had to be safety for those in storms.

With the membership now directed outward in mission, we focused our attention on those folk who lived near us who had no church affiliation or connection. We wanted to reach the people that Jesus came to reach. Jesus said, "I have come to seek and to save the lost" (Luke 19:10). We made it our goal to reach out to people who had no church family, who called no congregation their own. We wanted to reach out to those who wanted more, who were hungry for meaning and purpose in life.

To reach those in darkness, we made it our goal to be light, the light of Christ shining through us at every opportunity. We wanted to be bright, life-giving light. We wanted the house of worship to be warm, lit with God's love as it flows out of each person.

For those in need of safety, we offered a place where the most wounded would feel safe. The poor would be cared for, those in prison would be visited, and families in crisis could receive care and counseling. Marriage and family were priorities. And those who had other needs would be able to work with us to help buy food, redo their homes, care for their cars, as well as find care for their souls.

We were intentional about issues of safety and hospitality. We were clear that many in our midst came from abusive situations; many were survivors of life's cruelest deeds. We offered small groups as places where people could come to a home setting and in that setting, find care and love. We specialized in counseling, offering peer counseling support groups as well as hosting a counseling clinic in the church building. We offered AA for youth and young adults led by a member of the congregation who has been on the wrong side of the law and addicted to alcohol. But he had found new life in Christ, life that sustained him through jail.

After a few years, we saw that our mission statement did not really express what many thought God wanted us to do. We were growing and, in our growth, recognized we had a more intense purpose for our existence. By 1993, it became clear that God was calling us to reach the people around us with God's love. We felt urged to help as many as we could to know Jesus personally, experientially, and transformationally. Our focus needed to be more precise so we changed the mission statement to read: *that all might know Jesus.*

We knew why we were here: We wanted everyone to know Jesus. We did not want people to know *about* Jesus; we wanted people to *know* Jesus. How could we bring this about? We needed a vision statement. A vision statement would answer the question "how are we going to accomplish the mission of the church?" We found that our old mission statement, now deeply ingrained in all of us, contained much of our current vision. We would help all people to know Jesus by nurturing believers in Jesus Christ and by being light for any in darkness and safety for any in storms. This would affirm the overriding point of our existence, our reason for being, *that all might know Jesus.*

None of this happened overnight. It took three years to change the major committees of the church. First, I had to change the nominations committee, which nominated other people for the other committees. I insisted that no one could go back on the committee after serving a three-year term. In three years, I had the right mix in the nominations committee to begin overthrowing the power brokers in the other committees. And we kept praying. Walt Kallestad taught me to pray a very simple prayer about these matters: "Lord, revive them or remove them."[2] We saw many prayers answered. Within three years, the power brokers who were left were either outnumbered or had a drastic change of heart. One of the strongest members of the East Canton congregation experienced a change of heart regarding the new direction and the new people. He said to me one day, "I do not like the changes, but I like the new people." He caught a glimpse of the vision, understood the mission, and then could help other people understand the value in the congregation's new direction. He became one of the most positive forces for change in the church. He was a bridge builder between those who resisted change and those who were ready for more and more change. He was an insider who saw the Lord's hand in all of this and who knew that the growth meant more and more people would come to know the saving grace of Jesus Christ. He also knew more and more families would be helped, more and more youth would be reached before they made drastic mistakes, and more and more children would find a place of safety. The end result would be a congregation stronger than ever before. He could turn over control to the next generation, knowing that the congregation his great-grandfather helped found would remain for his great-grandchildren.

The Envisioning Team Process

As believers came to understand the joy of life in Jesus, people were touched by God's love. As people were touched, more small groups were started. As the number of small groups increased, we reached even more people, and worship attendance continued to grow.

As people grew in Christ, we taught them about their spiritual gifts. We wanted each person to discover and to use his or her gifts as soon as possible. To make the most of our situation and to fulfill the mission statement, we needed a new operational structure. The process of committees kept change from occurring. So we tried a new format for the administrative aspects of the church. We abolished most of the committees and formed an Envisioning Team composed of two subteams: Empowerment (helping believers grow—the nurture part of our vision statement) and Outreach (light and safety—the evangelistic and social justice aspect of the vision statement). Anyone could join the Envisioning Team. All you had to do was take the Spiritual Gifts Inventory. The new people did not bat an eye. The old control fanatics got angry and pouted, and some refused to take the inventory. We permitted those who would not take the inventory to attend the meetings. They were outnumbered, and gradually fewer of them came to the meetings. It was their loss.

Anyone could suggest an idea. There were no "no" votes! You could not vote against an idea. If you had the idea, it was the team's job to help you refine it, pay for it, and bring it about. After a three-month trial period, we voted not to go back to the old form. No, it was not in the *Discipline*,[3] but it worked and will work whenever you can trust the Christians you sit with. If you cannot trust each other, find a place with people you can trust.

This new format was created so that everything we did would be brought under the umbrella of the mission statement. The two subteams were given permission to do anything that would fulfill the mission of the church. There were no boards or committees they had to report to. The guidelines were simple: If you can dream it and it would help others "know Jesus," the Envisioning Team was obligated to help you raise the needed resources of time, people, and money. Creativity exploded as people were freed to dream and to envision the many ways God could use them.

The format for the Envisioning Team meeting took this form: Once a month, all who had taken a Spiritual Gifts Inventory met together for ninety minutes. We began each meeting in prayer. After a short teaching time, each group set up chairs around tables and began dreaming or brainstorming. What could these people do that would fulfill the mission and, at the same time, help accomplish our goals as part of this particular subteam of the Envisioning Team? Each month, someone new oversaw the process in each subteam. Someone else took notes. Notes were compiled and given to the church secretary the next day. The church secretary produced the "minutes" of the discussions for the next month's meeting. Ongoing projects were discussed first. Each project had two coordinators who were responsible for each project as well as for the evaluation of the project at its completion. The results of this process were as follows:

Empowerment—Anything that helped believers live for Jesus was fair game. This included discipleship, worship opportunities, prayer seminars, adult and children vacation Bible school, youth and children's programs, choirs, small groups, regional events, becoming a teaching congregation, spiritual enrichment weekends, retreats, walks to Emmaus, guest speakers, yearly events, evangelistic events, Bible studies, sermon series, and more.

Outreach—Anything that was light for those in darkness and safety for those in storms was planned and brought to completion. This took the form of women safety days, parish nurse, Karate for Christ, line dancing, AA for youth and adults, marriage enrichment, wild game dinners, care for cars events, Habitat for Humanity, CROP (Christian Rural Overseas Program), Bring-a-Friend Sunday, Care-for-Your-Neighbor Day, election events, Christian concerts, support for the local Christian school, Christian arts series, multiple services, a monthly food co-op, and many more.

At the end of each Envisioning Team gathering, tasks were assigned and projects not completed or attempted were put on the "to-do list" for consideration at the next month's meeting. Someone else was asked to supervise the next month's gathering. We gathered the two subteams back for ten minutes of debriefing, paying particular attention to the upcoming events from each circle and coordinating these events on the general calendar. We prayed together and went home charged up with all the possibilities that lie ahead. Sometimes we were overwhelmed with all that could be accomplished if we had the time.

How Can You Do This?

I frequently am asked how a local church can do this. I think it is difficult to come to but worth the effort. Here is how we did it.

1. We formed a group of core leaders who had a heart for ministry and who wanted this congregation to grow. We spent time together, teaching them, covering the basics, and praying together. We modeled small groups to them, giving them a firsthand picture of what small groups look like. We introduced them to other congregations that were growing so we might learn from others. We gave them everything we could find that was helpful. We passed all the good books we were reading to them. We took them to "church growth seminars." We pushed them to pray about being all they could be for God.

2. We worked with the Nominations Committee (in the early years we had committees) to have more visionary people appointed to every committee. If there was a committee in the church that did not relate to the mission of the church, we did not waste people filling those committees.

3. We taught at Administrative Council meetings and broke them up into small groups to help them dream and envision ministry possibilities.

4. We refused to allow the Personnel (Pastor Parish Relations) Committee to be the "whipping" committee of the church. If someone had a problem with the pas-

tor, he or she was to do the biblical thing of seeing the pastor (see Matt. 18:15-17). If you cannot say it to the pastor in person, do not say it. This forced people to grow up.

5. We asked the Official Body (our Administrative Council) to suspend the normal committee process for three months so we could experiment with the Envisioning Team format. In this three-month period there would be no "no" votes.

6. We removed the issue of money (a big control issue) by removing the treasurer's report from the Envisioning Team meeting. The report was typed and available. But unless we were broke, we were not going to spend our time worrying about money. *Money is never the issue.* God will always supply unless you worry about money and keep a firm grip on it. Then, like holding a water hose shut, the supply dwindles. Only dying churches fret about money. If you take your eyes off the account and focus on the people God has called you to reach with the love of Christ, God will take care of you. If you do not reach and love others for Jesus, why should God take care of you? I do not believe God is concerned with unproductive congregations. Why waste anyone else's time?

7. As more people came, we trained more people for their ministries. As you grow, you have to keep up with the need for leaders. To have effective leaders, you must spend time with them, mentor them, and grow them.

8. We worked with the "powers" (District Superintendent and Bishop) to assure the longevity of the pastoral appointment because longevity is a factor. It is clear that long-term pastorates are essential to growth. It took almost three years to win the trust of the people at East Canton. It took another three years to help them move from a "country club" to a "mission-oriented

congregation." It took another three years to convince them that ministry is "everyone's privilege" and not the job of the "paid Christian." Without longevity in the pastorate, turnarounds are impossible to achieve let alone sustain. When I consult with other congregations, one of the first questions I ask the pastor (pastoral staff) is: "Are you willing to stay ten more years?" I am a firm believer in not fixing things that are not broken. I was blessed to have the support of my District Superintendents in this process. I know they persuasively argued for my continued tenure at East Canton. Without their support, the longevity necessary for a turnaround would not have occurred.

SIX

Lever 3: Indigenous[1] Worship

Look around the congregation you worship in today. How many people are between the ages of fourteen and thirty-five? In most congregations, a large part of these generations have been lost. Like the Baby Boomers (those born between 1946 and 1959), these other generations may begin to return to our congregations when they have children. However, most studies show that these generations do not have a "Christian memory," that is, they are pre-Christian people. They never have been to worship and do not know what Christians believe. They find Christian worship repressive, irrelevant, and boring. So the talk of a "return" is, in my opinion, wishful thinking.

At East Canton in 1986, there were very few people in the fourteen to thirty-five age group. A few Baby Boomer families were bringing their children for "baptism." They would disappear and were seen again around Christmas and Easter. Who can blame them?

The worship service at East Canton in 1986 was vintage 1959. The songs were the same ones they had heard years ago in Sunday school. The order of the service, the words, and the music did little for them. There was a responsive call to worship, the obligatory three hymns, and pastoral drone—I mean prayer. The prayers were canned and empty. The Lord's Prayer was said each week in under 23.5

seconds, and the Apostles' Creed recited from memory in under 45 seconds. The entire event just dripped with meaning. The message was the highlight of the day. You could tell people expected to relax and be put to sleep. You are right that this is a slight exaggeration. The truth would have been even more boring.

Those raised in the church did not know any different. "We have always done it this way," they would say. Those not raised in the church but occasionally visited, found the order boring, the content confusing, the songs difficult, and the process irrelevant to them and their needs. This was a twice-a-year agony to be avoided. I agreed with them. I believe it is a sin to bore people. It is even worse to have the most wonderful news ever heard but wrap that message up in the dullest form you can for tradition's sake, while you bore and put off real people who come searching and longing for meaning in their torn-up lives.

LEADERSHIP TIP
More pastors have lost their parishes by changing the style of worship than for any other reason.
—Bill Easum

So we began to experiment and to change the content and style of the Sunday morning worship service. This was 1987, and everyone told us "you can't do that, you can't change the order of worship. You have to keep things like they have always been." We knew if we did not change the style and format of worship it would kill us, bore our children, and worse, keep this congregation irrelevant to people who needed the hope that only Jesus offers.

We also knew those raised in the church would resist changes, so we measured the amount of change we could try each week. We began by changing the format of the worship service on the second Sunday of the month. On that Sunday, we added praise choruses. We added personal interviews with people who had recently encountered the living Christ and had moving stories of God with them in times of pain as well as joy. We enlisted other people to "do" the service (lead songs, lead prayers, read scripture, and so on).

I sat with my family in the congregation. I hung up all the vestiges that separate clergy from laity. I put the robe in mothballs. I left the pulpit and even moved it from the center of the stage. Eventually I stopped wearing a tie, came casually dressed, and encouraged others to do the same. These were vast changes. Sure, people resisted. It was sacrilegious to come to church casually dressed. Pastors ought to wear robes to maintain a contrived, artificial distinction. We don't like this new music. Why don't we say the Lord's Prayer? Why don't we recite the creeds?

What could not be argued with was the success. We experienced growth. On the second Sunday of the month, more people visited and liked the less formal services. They liked the blend of tradition and innovation. They liked the songs, both praise choruses and hymns, because we kept everything upbeat. There were more people, and the offerings were larger. That really caught the attention of some.

By fall 1987, I chose sermon series on topics relevant to daily living. Each series was directly related to life issues and felt needs that the people were facing.[2] Each message was geared for practical instruction rather than filled with religious jargon. We emphasized the Bible, the reality of God's love in Jesus, the possibility of transformation, and the need for a direct relationship with Jesus Christ. But we also addressed real issues. We did not give history lessons, berate anyone, or focus on issues that were not relevant to life, right here, right now.

Moving from the Head to the Heart

Playing my guitar in worship was a radical shift. I taught the congregation songs that spoke to the heart instead of just to the head. I taught them songs that spoke of majesty and love of God—songs like "Holy Ground," "Majesty," and "In Moments Like These." We sang the songs until we knew them by heart and then turned the song into a prayer. We sang directly to Jesus, using that wonderful gift of visualization. Those under fifty generally loved the worship and requested to sing these songs more often. Those over fifty generally did not like singing the same words over and over. I asked the organist to play the piano. Since the church was not European, it should not act like it is.[3] We left out the creeds and the Lord's Prayer; we even removed the pastoral prayer. Instead, we asked people to turn to those near them and pray for them and their needs right then and there, before God and everyone.

Sure, people complained. It wasn't church like this. Why don't we say the Lord's Prayer? Why don't we say the creed? Why don't we do things the way we always did? I pointed out to them that on the Sundays when we were more relaxed we attracted more people. I asked them if what they had been doing was so great, why was this building, now over 150 years old, still able to hold all the people with ample room?

In 1988, we attempted a Saturday night worship service that rotated between the two congregations on the charge. This worship service was much more contemporary than anything we did on Sunday morning. Mostly young people came, and it was a struggle for them as most were involved in Sunday morning programs and services as well. We just were not large enough to have three services. We eventually stopped the Saturday night service, took what we learned from it, and gradually implemented changes into the Sunday morning service. For example, we broke people into small groups to pray for each other. Once a month, we had no order of service, but we sang a lot, prayed a lot, and taught the Bible. When there were people in need, we asked if they were willing to come forward for prayer and asked all of those who had gifts in healing, intercession, faith, or mercy to pray for these people. Other instruments were used, notably the piano, flute, and guitar. And we grew even more.

By 1993, our typical worship service had a new look. People were eager to greet you (in the parking lot, at the front door, at the hospitality center, at the name tag desk, and in the sanctuary). Upon entering the sanctuary, you could hear music. Fifteen minutes before the service, the singing began. Members of the choir or those with spiritual gifts in music led the songs.

At the time the service was advertised to start, we started with a few announcements (thirty to sixty seconds) and then asked people to get up and greet each other. As they were milling about, we began the music. We usually sang two upbeat songs followed by a mellow, more meditative song. We sang hymns and choruses. After singing, we had a time to share joys and testimonies: "What has God done for you this week?" These were practical, nonrehearsed stories from people who had encountered the living God in their lives. It was always a comfort to hear how God had helped others during the week. How moving it was to hear of a coworker led to Christ or of someone able to pray for a customer at the local floral shop. After "joys," we moved to prayer. Sometimes people would share particular prayer requests. Most times we would just pray, aloud, together. That's right, WE would pray! Anyone was welcomed to raise his or her voice and share a prayer. No one was forced, but everyone was invited. It took a while to get comfortable going to a microphone to pray. We even had people who would bring a microphone to you if you could not get up. Occasionally we broke up in small groups of two to five people to pray for each other. Regularly we would ask people with a special need for healing or comfort to come to the front of the room where others would gather about them, lay hands on them, and pray for them (James 4:6).

Following our prayer time, the worship team took over again and led in singing choruses for ten to fifteen more minutes. The worship leader shared her heart about God's love and how God's love related to the songs we sang. After the singing, one member of the worship team prayed for the morning teaching. Except when playing the guitar, I sat with my family. Imagine a pastor sitting with his or her family during worship. It's almost sacrilegious to some but is a practice I keep to this day. I do not need to be in front of everyone. I need to be close to my family, next to my wife, daughter, and son. As pastor, I need to empower and equip all willing believers to use their spiritual gifts.

Following the choruses, I taught on practical topics such as "How to Make Your Marriage Affair Proof" or "How to Raise Godly Children" or "Caught, Not Taught—Sharing the Love of Jesus" or "Embracing Your Anger Without Blowing Your Top." The teaching time was usually followed by a time for questions or commitment, dedication, and responding to the call of God in one's life. Rarely were people asked to "come on down!" Instead, they were asked to go to the back of the sanctuary and into the prayer room after worship to meet with people waiting for them. God regularly touched people in real ways. Lives were regularly touched by God's presence. Touched lives turned into changed lives.

The closing song always related to the theme. It summed up the positive aspects of the message and encouraged each person to make a commitment to live for Jesus to a greater degree than previously.

If after the service you had a particular need for prayer, there were people gathered in the prayer room to listen and pray for you. Because I had two congregations some miles apart, I rarely was able to stay. Other leaders in the congregation did the ministry that God had called them to do.

As people left the sanctuary, music continued to play. God was not finished with us just because the clock said it was time to go. Many times real ministry occurred after the service ended. Real people, really called and really gifted, would seek out those in need and care for them.

Each week the service seemed to grow in depth, with a deeper sense of God's presence. This happened because all were empowered and given permission to use their gifts. From the greeters in the parking lot, to the opening song leader, to the worship leader, to the musicians, each person was given permission to use his or her gifts. As a result, I had a lot of energy for teaching. I did not have to worry about the service. Each part of it was led by competent, gifted persons. Let me introduce two of them.

Laureen

Laureen was from a family that lived on a working farm. She loved to play the piano and organ for worship, and she loved to be a part of the worship of God. It was her gift to pick the music that would fit with each series of talks. Best of all, she was teachable and loved serving God. Although classically trained, she was able to play both sides of the field. We could sing some of the hardest classical works, and we could sing some of the most moving contemporary choruses. Each week, Laureen gave her all, her best. Her playing was not too slow, not too fast, and always sensitive to God moving among us. She was a heart person and did not require much prodding from me for her to trust God and to allow God to lead her. As the congregation grew, I knew she would seek God when choosing the music, so I gave her permission to pick the songs each week. I supplied her the topics I was going to address, and she would pick the songs and the special numbers and arrange for choir anthems. Each Sunday was a special gift. Many times I looked over at her as the worship team led songs and saw tears running down her cheeks.

What a contrast to so many situations where "right music" is more important than touching lives for God. So often professional musicians and others say to me, "How long will we have to play *that* music before these people like *good* music?" I say, how long will our congregations be held hostage to a one-size-fits-all mentality? How blessed East Canton was to have a person who could play classically and who had her heart open for God, too. It is time for churches to learn that God speaks in different languages and musical styles in different ways to reach different people with the unchanging good news of Jesus Christ.

Pam

Pam was the mother of four and a schoolteacher who had a heart for worship. To my knowledge, she was never trained in contemporary worship and had no advanced degrees in theology or music, but she knew what it meant to stand honestly before God. Week after week, Pam helped us experience God's presence in ways that spoke to our hearts and spoke of God's great love for us. Pam allowed God to use her as a light for many who were in darkness. And through the various experiences of her life, she was able to communicate how safe we really are in God's hands. Often as we sang, Pam encouraged us to surrender more of our lives to God. She would encourage us to risk giving God our hearts, our worries, our fears. As I looked about the congregation, I saw hearts melting and lives changed by the touch of the Jesus.

While many pastors may lose their parishes for suggesting changes to the worship style, it is crucial to offer varied styles of worship if we are to be relevant to the vast majority of people who live around us. "Traditional" or "contemporary" is not really the issue. Let's get to the crux of the issue. Does our worship speak the language of the people we want to reach? Does our worship result in changed lives? Indigenous worship that changes lives is what is important, not the style that worship takes.

SEVEN

Lever 4: Growth Groups[1]

As the growth in worship attendance continued, we were not able to provide a caring connection for all the new people, let alone for all of those who had been faithful followers and supporters of the congregation. With 140-plus people in worship at East Canton and 100-plus people in worship at Windfall, providing chaplaincy care for all those people was simply beyond my time, desires, and abilities. At the time, the congregations were not able or willing to hire additional staff, not even a part-time secretary. The small-church mentality played a large role here. It is so hard to help people see that at 140-plus people in worship, our worship attendance was larger than it is in 80 percent of all Protestant churches in America.

As we reached higher worship attendance numbers, the quality of care suffered. If I had attempted to do all the pastoral care I would have eventually burned out, run out of steam, and been forced to give up. Yes, there were some who thought I should be in each home each year. Yes, there were some who were angry that I would not visit regularly. These tended to be the same vocal minority that would oppose every new idea. So, what were we to do to care for regular attendees and visitors as well as for those who were hurting in our mission area?

From what I saw in the New Testament, Christian believers were providing care for others from the beginning. There were even special groups of people who were called to care for those with special needs (Acts 7). The majority of the care came about as people met in homes where they would pray for each other, study together, and worship together (Acts 20:20). In Acts, believers were "devoted to each other." Why would that not work here? Why couldn't we train growth group leaders and begin small groups? These small groups would care, pray, study, and learn to be devoted to each other. It looked like this pattern worked in the early church, and why would it not work now?

LEADERSHIP TIP

In the New Testament, the primary unit of care was the home-based small group.

Growth groups were not a new idea to me. In 1971, only a few months after beginning a new life in Jesus Christ, I was blessed to participate in a growth group experience (but it was not known to us as such). Four to six high-school students met weekly in the sanctuary of a United Methodist church. Each Wednesday night at 9:00, we gathered to pray, share, sing, and study the Bible. We did not have a clue what we were doing, but this was life for us. It was an appointment none of us would miss. It was a wonderful way to learn from others, to share our lives (the good, the bad, and the ugly) with one another. We held one another's lives in unconditional acceptance. We came to the Bible as beginners and allowed the text to speak to us. I began looking for and cultivating this experience everywhere I went—college, seminary, and into the parish. This became a formational pattern in my life. A few people gathering together for one hour to pray, share, sing, study, love, grow, and encourage others to be contagious for Jesus is beneficial beyond measure. It has been a life-giving experience.

At East Canton, growth groups became the backbone that supported and allowed our growth to continue by providing quality care to many people. Growth groups touched all areas of life, and the leaders of each group provided quality care for those who attended their groups on a weekly basis. On any given week, there were 100-plus people in growth groups in the East Canton area. Each person was cared for, loved, prayed for, nurtured, and encouraged. Each person was encouraged to invite more people to the group. Many found their way from the growth groups to the worship services. One pastor never could have accomplished that much.

We started growth groups by modeling what a growth group looked like. For two years we conducted growth groups that were open to anyone. These groups met on various days of the week and at different times of the day. We urged those attending the growth groups to start new groups in their homes. As the participants were exposed to small-group dynamics, we developed a strategy to start growth groups in this congregation. After two years of modeling and teaching, growth groups were planted all over the area.

There would be a person in each group who demonstrated the gift of a group leader. We would approach this person and ask him or her to prayerfully consider leading a group. Their usual response was, "I can't do that." We would respond, "We think you can. You have all the tools you need. You have the life witness, you know it will bless others, and we believe God is calling you to this. Please pray about this." The individual would say, "I will pray, but I do not think it will work. I do not think I have the skill, knowledge, time, or energy. But I will pray and let you know."

You would have thought we were asking that person to go on a top secret mission to Mars. All we asked that person to do was to begin a growth group in the neighborhood, invite a few people from the congregation and a few from the neighborhood, and gather together once a week. But again, this was different; this was change. This was different from anything they had ever done before. Change, as we all know, is scary. Could they trust God with this?

For those who responded positively to the call to leadership, we developed a plan for them to get started. The plan worked well with all the groups we started. When we read Dale Galloway's material,[2] we saw that what we were doing he had already refined and made more usable. It was no problem to switch from our homegrown plan to Galloway's material. It really helped us.

The Plan

First, pray for seven to ten names of people God wants to have at your small group. Make sure you invite people who do not attend church or who do not know much about God or Jesus.

Second, pray for these people every day for two weeks.

Third, find a host or hostess (someone with the gift of hospitality) who will open his or her home and be hospitable to others.

Fourth, set a time and a place for the small group.

Fifth, find someone who will lead the study. Usually this is the same person who feels called to host the group.

Sixth, at the end of two weeks of prayer, invite the people you have been praying for to the host or hostess's house for coffee and cake. Share the idea with them about the small group over the phone. Make sure you invite people who do not have a church home.

Seventh, remember the mission is *that all might know Jesus*, and do all you can to be light and safety. Trust is imperative. The goal of growth groups, like any project at East Canton, was to fulfill the mission to which God had called us. To accomplish this, growth groups had to be intentional about the mission.

Eighth, remember that the object is to create more growth groups to care for more people, so each group needs to birth new groups on a regular basis. Once the group gets to eight or ten people, begin planning to birth two groups from the original one. (This step was the one that gave us the most trouble.)

Ninth, keep the format of each group uniform. In the hour each group met, we attempted to break down the time into three sections: twenty minutes of Bible study, twenty minutes of sharing, and twenty minutes of prayer.

Tenth, begin and end on time. Do not ask people to stay longer than the hour.

Joey

Joey was a retired elementary school teacher. Her husband had recently died, and she wanted to be more involved in sharing God's love with others. She had attended one of my growth groups and one day said to me, "I'd really like to start a group in my home, but I'm a little scared." So we talked and prayed about "the plan." Joey followed the instructions. She called me two weeks later in tears. She had prayed, gotten the names, and called the first two names on her list. Both people told her "no way." Now what? I told her to call the other names and then call me back. She called back that night in jubilation. The others had said yes. The first two, when they heard that the others said yes, called Joey to ask if they could come.

A men's group started in a similar fashion. God was growing our groups. We were obviously reaching a great need in the lives of many. Lou started a group fifteen miles from the church. Ira and Lyle had one of the largest groups, sometimes with fifteen to eighteen men attending.

Lessons Learned the Hard Way

We attempted to keep the groups small, between eight to ten people, but they usually grew past that size. The biggest obstacle was convincing people to birth new groups. After meeting together for a few months, the groups became major centers of care and love. People were hungry for that kind of relational encounter. The groups continued to grow. People were so loved and accepted in their growth group that they would not want to leave it. Eventually, the group grew too large, the atmosphere changed, and trust was hard to maintain in a large group (over ten) where people did not consistently attend. So people dropped out. Some of these groups grew too large and lost 25 percent or more of the people, who eventually stopped attending any group.

This was my problem, and I learned valuable lessons the hard way. I made three big mistakes:

1. Failure to meet with the group leaders regularly to continue mentoring them. Once a quarter was not good enough.
2. Not demonstrating how to birth new groups in ways that were helpful. I would suggest that they do this but did not mentor this process or coach them through it. Consequently most of the small groups grew too big and then lost people who did not rejoin another small group.
3. Not stressing that the main reason for the groups was to reach the unchurched. Consequently, some groups were composed entirely of churched people. The lack

of seekers—unchurched or "pre-Christian" people—
hurt the groups by neglecting the infusion of new
blood in the small groups.

Don't make these mistakes!

Success Stories

Overall, the growth groups involved many people who
were given the very best of care. This network kept many
people connected to a source of life that enabled them to go
through difficult times. Let me tell you about one incident
that occurred while I was out of town.

Dawn was a young mother who lived in the nearby
town. Her husband, Ken, was a trucker, on the road a lot,
but usually home each weekend. Dawn and Ken began
attending East Canton with their children and were soon in
the middle of small groups (as well as everything else).
Dawn attended the trainings and began hosting a growth
group in her home. She invited friends, neighbors, and others she knew to the group. One of those people was Kris.

Kris had a difficult life. Marriage was hard. Life was
hard. Kris began attending the small group that met at
Dawn's home. Gradually Kris came to worship. Eventually
her husband and family started attending worship.

One day Kris got a call that her father had died. What
was she to do? She called Dawn. Dawn and others from her
small group showed up at Kris's door. Dawn and members
of the small group stayed at Kris's home to wait for her children to get home from school. They cleaned her house and
made supper so when her husband got home, he and the
children would have something to eat. They stayed with
Kris for the next several days. They went to the funeral with
her, supported her in prayer, and cared for her and her family. When I got back into town a few days later, I was told

about this. There was nothing for me to do because Dawn and her small group did it all. These people cared for another human being with no reservations. They gave her life, giving of themselves. What a difference the presence of caring others makes in our lives. The next Sunday in worship, Kris stood and said, "I have never known love like this in my life."

I am not sure who learned the most, Kris, Dawn, or me. We all learned that God is ready and able to use people if they will allow God to use them as they take the risk in faith to follow where he leads. So often pastors burn out attempting to do everything and to be there for everyone. This robs the laity of their ministries, burns out the pastoral leadership, and perpetuates the lie that clergy can and laity cannot.

What Kris learned that day will carry her through life: There are people who do care, who know Jesus Christ and seek to live for him, who drop their busy schedules to help. They do not stand far off and offer pious words. They come to clean your house, and even your bathroom. They fix meals, watch your children, and do your laundry. They stand with you at the casket of your father and pray that God will be your strength. They listen. They care. Dawn will never be ordained, but she could be my pastor any day of the week!

Mark

Mark[3] was single, fresh out of college, and making a living as a carpenter. He was alive for Christ. Mark began a growth group by inviting all the people who lived near him to gather each week. This intergenerational group was composed of single men and women, married couples, teenagers, and even two younger children. What a collection! They met each week; they prayed, cared, loved each other, and the group grew in many ways. Mark was their pastor, their care giver. He was in their lives each week. One of the single people and a few of the teens and children wanted to be baptized. Mark came to me and said, "Can you do a baptism soon? I have all these people who are asking to be baptized." I said, "Why should I do this? Why don't you do it?" He gave me all the reasons why pastors have to do "religious" stuff. For me, the Gospel of Matthew 28:20 says, "Go into all the world and make disciples, baptizing them in the name of the Father and of the Son and of the Holy Spirit, teaching them all I commanded you." We allow people to reach their neighbors with the good news. We allow all people to make disciples. We allow all people to teach. Why not allow all people to baptize? I do! I told him I would assist, but he would do it. We went to the pond, and Mark baptized them. It was a great day!

Small groups taught us that life lived with the support of a few caring people is really full of adventure. With all the new people in our groups, there were baptisms and dedications, new faces, and lots and lots of questions about life and God each week. You cannot spend your days complaining about the pastor's sermon when that new person in your group has just come to Christ and has so many questions that you do not have any clues about. So you dig in the Word, you share your life, and you pray. You do not have time to complain about the color of the paint in the bathroom when you are so busy helping new Christians face the struggles of living by faith or when you are caring for those who face death or when you are sharing the wonderful news of God's love with that neighbor who has never heard Jesus' name except in cursing. Congregational life takes on new meaning. Ralph Neighbour says, cells or growth groups "are a return to a life style which has been bastardized by centuries of unbiblical, crusted traditions. The cell group is not just a portion of church life, to be clustered with a dozen other organizations. It is church life; and when it properly exists, all other competing structures are neither needed nor valid."[4]

Joey, Lou, Ira, Lyle, Dawn, and Mark. Each one was just a normal person using his or her gifts to help others know the wonderful love of Jesus Christ. Each one learned more lessons about living for Jesus as leaders of small groups than in attending Sunday school. The result was more people active in vital life-changing ministries. Each person became more alive and in tune with God's intentions.

We had other growth groups as well. Some were for couples that met on Friday nights. Others were for older people. There were multigenerational groups, women's groups, and youth groups. Some of these groups met only from September to May. Some would meet for six to eight weeks and then close. Some never got off the ground. Growth groups are avenues for Christians to learn about their spiritual gifts, to experiment using those gifts, and to learn how to lead pre-Christian people into a life-changing relationship with Jesus Christ. Growth groups are living on the edge of adventure. Growth groups are a crucial lever in the process of turning a church around.

As pastor, I was freed from so many "pastoral care" issues. This enabled me to use my gifts as well. I could spend more time in the prisons. I could spend time in the counseling room. I could spend time with the leaders, praying, planning, and dreaming. And I could spend time with my family.

EIGHT

Lever 5: Membership That Means Something

As East Canton grew, more people came to know the love of God in Jesus Christ. Many of these individuals asked to be baptized. At East Canton, adults were baptized more frequently than youth or children. Some people, many from a more traditional upbringing, asked to "join" the church. Many of the hard living people who were attracted to the church came regularly but did not want to join, did not want "to be obligated." I did not blame them. I often wondered what it meant to join the church. I was never a "joiner" myself, like so many Boomers. Fraternities, civic groups, and churches all want people to become "members," but for what reason? Usually it is to enlist help to further their cause, keep the group running, pay for the upkeep of the building, or demonstrate that this group is the biggest or best. None of those reasons appealed much to me or to many around East Canton.

LEADERSHIP TIP

Membership has to mean more than having a name on the roll book.

In 1986, there were many members on the roll who never or rarely showed their faces at any congregational gathering.[1] I did not want more inactive people on the roll book. Likewise, I did not want to turn away people who really wanted to commit themselves to Jesus Christ. Added names on the roll meant added expense, added responsibility, and added trouble.

To make membership mean something, we plotted a course that would take us in two directions. First, membership carried "responsibility." If new people were to go through a process to be members and take responsibility for their commitments, then the people already on the membership roll had to take seriously the meaning of membership. To return membership to its meaningful place, we removed every inactive member from the roll so that those on the roll were those who did more than show up once or twice a year. Second, new members would have to go through a "process," in which we could determine who really shared the passion and the mission of the congregation (what many are calling the DNA[2]).

The Removing Process

If you were a member of East Canton and

1. were not confined to your home or a nursing home,
2. were not confined to a hospital bed,
3. were not active in worship, and
4. did not contribute to the life of the congregation by:
   a. prayerfully supporting the ongoing ministries,
   b. attending worship, and
   c. contributing financially to the operational expenses of ministry

then we gave you the option of renewing your vows or withdrawing your membership. In the United Methodist system, you were placed on a three-year list. Each year, you were sent a letter or received a phone call. The purpose of the contact was to invite you to return to worship. Included in the letter was a stamped, addressed postcard. The post-card gave you two options:

Option one: Please keep my name on the rolls. I dedicate myself to East Canton congregation by supporting it with my prayers, presence, service, and tithes.

Option two: Please remove my name.

If we did not get the card back, we placed the name in the three-year removal list.

After three years of contact with no commitment or no response, we removed the name from the membership roll. In a few years, we reduced the membership from 237 to 118. Attendance at worship during this same time went from 55 to 140.

Some thought we should meet face to face with the people on the three-year list. This was impossible because many of these people no longer lived in the community or state. After talking to many people who had tried this approach, we decided this would be a poor use of our time. On each card there was an opportunity to make an appointment to talk to someone about membership concerns. No one ever called to make an appointment.

The Joining Process

We thought about the commitment we expected people to make when wanting membership at East Canton. To what were they committing? What would *membership that means something* look like?

We determined this process would consist of two phases. The first phase began with a one-hour gathering held once a month, usually on a Sunday afternoon or evening. This was an informal meeting of anyone thinking about membership. In this first session, we covered what we called "the six essential elements of membership." In order to become a member at East Canton, you had to agree to make these six conditions a priority in your life. This would be your membership covenant, a pledge between you and God and this particular Body of Christ.

The second phase of this process was an individual interview session with the pastor. During the interview, I asked each person about his or her personal faith journey and whether or not he or she could support the mission, vision, and values of the East Canton congregation.

Phase 1: Six Conditions of Meaningful Membership

1. An Abiding, Personal Relationship with Jesus Christ

A personal relationship with Jesus Christ is essential. Not did they believe in God, but did they have a personal encounter with Jesus Christ? Did the person have a relationship with Jesus Christ? That is, did they know Jesus? Not just know about Jesus, but were they intimately aware of his presence and love in their lives? Were their "hearts strangely warmed"? Could they share the good news of God's grace with others? Did they know the love of God, and could they talk about God's love with others? Would they share their experience of God's love in a worship service? Having a personal relationship with Jesus Christ would demonstrate itself in a desire to care for and share with those who were not yet convinced of their need for Jesus Christ. Would they take a Spiritual Gifts Inventory and, based on the results, be willing to use their gifts in the mission and outreach of the congregation? Would they be willing to use their gifts so that others might know Jesus?

2. *Active Participation in a Growth Group*

To be a member, each person would have to promise to participate in a growth group on a regular basis, noting that every other week would be okay but that every week would be better. Growth groups were essential to the Christian care of the congregation. Would they seek to honor God by growing with a growth group?

3. *Regular, Personal Devotional Time*

Each person wishing to join would commit to a personal devotional life that included prayer for the local church and a time of daily personal study of Scripture. An emphasis was placed on prayer—corporate and individual—prayer retreats, and seminars.

4. *Stewardship of Time, Talents, and Tithe*

Each person would honor God by the stewardship of his or her time, talents, and financial resources. It would be expected that each person give at least four hours to God each week by attending growth groups, using spiritual gifts, and attending worship. Each person would honor God by using the talents, natural gifts, and spiritual gifts God gave in service to the mission of East Canton, *that all might know Jesus.* Each person would honor God by tithing, that is, a regular contribution of at least 10 percent of gross income each month. Some said they could not give 10 percent right away, but they would attempt to give more, upping their contribution 1 percent each year until they were at 10 percent. While money is always an issue for the yet-to-be convinced and for the religious, I rarely meet disciples who tithe but still worry about small things like money. As I learned from Walt Kallestad years ago, "Money is never the issue. The issue is always our faith."[3]

5. *Hands-on Mission Involvement*

Members must involve themselves in a mission project or take leadership for some mission of the congregation. They could be part of any mission-oriented project. Examples of available mission projects were: CROP, Habitat for

Humanity, and Operation Hugo (hurricane relief). Any mission project was acceptable as long as it fit the mission, vision, and value statements of the congregation.

6. Regular Attendance in Worship

It was expected that each person joining East Canton would be a regular worship attendee. When you were on vacation, we expected you to attend worship somewhere and then tell us all the wonderful things you learned from other congregations. If you were in town, we expected you to be present and to participate in worship.

Those who would consent to all six conditions could join the membership of the congregation. The actual joining occurred during worship. A vocal assent to each condition was given, and the congregation affirmed each new member and likewise made a commitment to help one another keep the conditions of this covenant. Pledging to support the six conditions of membership placed a person on the first steps toward leadership in the congregation.

Phase 2: The Individual Interview

I scheduled individual meetings with each person who indicated a willingness to embrace the six conditions of *membership that means something*. In these individual interviews, I asked pointed and direct questions in an attempt to discern if they had understood the mission, if they owned that mission, and if they would be willing to work toward the fulfillment of the mission (the DNA). I tried to make sure they knew what we expected. I also indicated that membership was not necessary to worship with us. If they did not feel they could commit themselves to the six conditions, that was between them and God. They were still part of the fellowship, and if they would be willing to take the Spiritual Gifts Inventory, they could attend the Envisioning Team.[4] However, unless they were willing to agree to the conditions for meaningful membership, they could not be lay pastors or growth group leaders.

Results

Many did not join, at least at first. Usually it was three or four months after the initial meeting before someone would grow to the place of making the kind of commitment we asked from those wanting to be "members."

Membership that means something is a commitment to some high goals.

Membership that means something was not to be entered into "lightly and unadvisedly."

Membership that means something was our attempt to make sure the leadership was growing by first making sure they:

1. had the passion for ministry and used the gifts God had so graciously given them to support and advance the ministry of the East Canton congregation,
2. would be involved in small groups,
3. would pray,
4. would tithe their time and resources,
5. would be directly involved in missions, and
6. would be regular in worship.

Many people came to a new relationship with Jesus Christ at this time. Many had been "in" the church for a long time but had never known a personal relationship with Jesus Christ. Many thought the pastor was the "paid Christian" and that if you "showed up, paid up, and shut up," you were doing all you could do.

One woman told me, "A previous pastor told me 'you can't ever know God or be assured you are going to heaven. You have to hope you die on a day when God is in a good mood.' " How anthropomorphic and immature. What fear that pastor placed in that good woman's heart. She spent her days sure you could not know God, experience God's love, or know God's forgiveness.

Some of those in the pews resisted this new emphasis. Many made sure they attended worship each week but would not go near a small group, take a Spiritual Gifts Inventory, or confess to knowing or not knowing Jesus Christ. That was fine, but those same people were upset that they were not listened to or placed in leadership roles. New outsiders were funneled into leadership while some longtimers were left behind. Some never got over it. But from my perspective, if Christians were not willing to grow up in Jesus Christ, why should those immature children be placed at the steering wheel of a car? What good reason could there be for allowing immature, "eternal" children to be in leadership roles? What adult would allow a four-year-old to drive a car?

The impact of having *membership that means something* cleared the way for those who were committed to move into leadership. Those outside the congregation knew we were serious and were no longer "playing" church. What a difference that made with the hard living people in our area. Hypocrite was not a label used to describe the new members or leaders.

The biggest advantage of this new approach was the influx of new life into the church and especially in the Envisioning Team. The joy of meeting with a team that was committed to the mission and wanted everyone to know Jesus was priceless. I was freed from baby-sitting and instead watched a mighty army going forth, telling the good news, seeing lives changed, and watching many people grow up right before my eyes. There is something really healthy about that. I was grateful for the opportunity to learn these lessons and to put them into practice, to see that this approach not only worked, but also brought about greater levels of faithfulness and dedication in the leadership and in many other people in the community.

NINE

Lever 6: Lay Pastoring

To prepare God's people for works of service [ministry], so that the body of Christ may be built up.

(Eph. 4:12 NIV)

It has been my experience that helping people find hope and a reason for life centered in the love of God in Jesus Christ is one of the most exciting and life-fulfilling aspects of existence. Ministry for me has always been more than holding the hands of people watching television. Ministry has always been more than standing on doorsteps, writing notes to people who were too ill to attend worship but were able to go bowling once a week. I had more in mind for ministry than doing all the ministry, being "the paid Christian," or playing "pastor fetch." Why can't all Christian people know the joy of sharing the good news with others? Why is this wonderful, dynamic slice of life not the right of each person who calls Jesus "Lord"? Why was it so deeply rooted in the church that pastors are the only people able to do ministry? This had to change. It is not helpful. It is not biblical. It no longer works. The challenge before me was to change this attitude in this local congregation and to free up each believer to live in the excitement and joy of sharing the good news of Jesus.

To begin making the necessary changes, I simply stopped

allowing others to believe this lie. Based on what I saw in Scripture, from my own experience, and from reason, I saw that this "tradition" had its roots in many crusty practices carried over from centuries ago that still plague the Body of Christ in the twenty-first century. I confronted the lie head on. I spoke against the artificial division of clergy and laity. I taught that, based on Ephesians 4:12, each and every believer has a ministry, a calling from God to discover and use his or her gifts that the Body of Christ might, in Paul's words, "reach unity in the faith and in the knowledge of the Son of God and become mature." I lived as an example of what that would look like. I stopped praying at public gatherings and asked other people to pray instead. I stopped dressing like I was different. I no longer wore backward collars (which the rich had worn in centuries gone by and which clergy adopted when they went out of style). I refused to allow people to call me "reverend" and would submit to the descriptive "gift" word, pastor. What I wanted to do was call each person by the gift God had given them, like Encourager Joyce, Evangelist Steve, Helper Nancy, and Teacher Ira. Soon, people got the hint and called me by my name. Sure, people still hoped I would play pastor fetch, called me reverend, and asked me to pray. But I would not play fetch, corrected them that I am not reverend or holy, and asked others to pray. I do not need you to think that I am holy and hope that one day I will use my gifts and you will use yours and, together, we can bring a generation to Jesus Christ. As long as I allow the lie to exist and foster that lie by different dress and different titles, I cannot expect other believers to free themselves from the lie that keeps them from being in ministry right now.

As I travel, I still encounter these artificial distinctions in almost every congregation I visit. No wonder. Look at what most of us were taught about pastoring by the church and seminaries over the last forty years.

Churches will be successful if the pastor will understand and practice the following three principles:

1. Good Preaching will attract people.
2. Good Pastoral Care will keep them coming.
3. Good Administration will ensure the success of the ministry [or was it the minister? And what is the measure you are using for success anyway?].

I realized that this thinking kept many people out of real ministry (leading others to Jesus Christ, discipleship). This thinking was the cause of burnout for many pastors around me as they overextended themselves in order to please their congregations and do all the ministry. In this pattern it would not take long for the pastors (and their families) to wind up bitter, worn out, and confused, with families resenting the church and congregations asking for more from the pastor.[1] Even in a local a nondenominational congregation, I saw a pastor limit the lay participation in ministry so he might be able to control everything happening, and maybe take credit for it as well.

I have found that as each believer discovers his or her spiritual gifts, prepares to use those gifts in ministry, and is given permission to carry out their ministry without having to jump through hoops, ministry opportunities explode. Incredible numbers of people are touched by God's love as the Body of Christ finds that its feet, hands, arms, and other parts really work. To help this process along, we developed a course of training called the Lay Pastor School.

True Pastors[2]

What was I to call all these people who I believed God had already given gifts for ministry and were willing to let me push them into ministry? They were pastors! They were the shepherds of this flock. Instead of jumping through numerous hoops on their way to ordination, they had been ordained by God, and it was my job to equip them, support them, and send them into the mission field—their community, their neighbors, right here, right now.

While they needed to be released to do their ministry, they first needed to be trained and then coached for ministry. We began a ten-week course to teach these pastors all we knew about ministry. We hoped this would propel them to venture forth into the ministries to which God was calling them. We were not disappointed.

The class time was divided into instructional time, experiential time, and a time for questions and answers. The training was open to anyone but targeted those who had found their way to the congregation, took seriously the six conditions of membership, and were demonstrating signs of spiritual giftedness. We began every class with worship and prayer. One training session was for two hours on Monday nights. One training session met on Wednesday mornings. The Monday night training in the first session had fifteen people from East Canton and ten people from neighboring congregations. The Wednesday group was smaller, with six people regularly attending. But remember, we were a small congregation in very rural north-central Pennsylvania.

Structure of the True Pastor's Course[3]

First Session: Discovering Your Ministry—Capturing God's Vision for Your Life

This was basically an overview and rationale for pastoring. We covered Loren B. Mead's *The Once and Future Church*[4] and Bill Easum's *Church Growth Handbook*[5] and saw the historical implications of our time. We learned about the basic responsibilities of pastors, their basic qualifications, the need for a positive attitude, and the fourfold work of a pastor (Ambassador, Shepherd, Missionary, Servant).

In this first session, we took a Spiritual Gifts Inventory and looked at the results and implications of that inventory. We divided people into groups according to their gifting and allowed them to discuss how they see God using their gifts in their lives. We asked them to pray that during the course of that week they all might find opportunities to use their gifts.

Second Session: Ambassador—Discovering Your Ministry of Care

Taking a lead from Paul's second letter to the church in Corinth, we looked at what it means to be an Ambassador for Christ (2 Cor. 5:17). The giving of care and, in fact, the entire process of being a pastor at East Canton was grounded in the mission *that all might know Jesus* as we were light for those in darkness and safety for those in storms. In the second half of the second session, we focused on the Ambassador qualities of a pastor. Those qualities are summed up for me in the word "care." We explored "What is care?" and how to extend that care to others. We learned specific techniques like "God-centered listening"[6] and how to discern Core-Conflict Relational Themes.[7] We practiced listening with each other and used fictional verbatim material to help people identify Core-Conflict themes. We learned how to listen with empathy and compassion. We used role-plays and then debriefed as a group, talking about the issues, the highlights, and the "mistakes" we make in our listening and our interventions.

Third Session: Shepherding, Feeding, and Tending of Sheep

Building on Jesus' conversation with Peter following the resurrection, we looked at what it means to love Jesus and therefore to be called to care for others who likewise love Jesus. The practical aspects of shepherding are teaching, tending, and leading. Using Psalm 23, we looked at each of these aspects in light of the responsibility of the pastor to care for the souls of other believers. Pastors were expected to be able to teach the Bible in small groups or other settings. We covered styles of teaching and how to facilitate meaningful discussions.

Fourth Session: Missionary, Evangelism, and Disciple Making

Jesus said, "Go therefore and make disciples of all nations" (Matt. 28:19). Bill Bright says, "The key starting point in bringing a loved one to Christ is prayer."[8] As missionaries seeking to bring many to Christ, we must begin by praying for those God is placing in our sphere of contact—coworkers, family members, as well as "chance" encounters. We reach out in genuine love relying on the Holy Spirit and simply are available to God for others. Disciple making begins at the point of contact with any person willing to grow and to learn about Jesus and the Christian life. The disciple-making process is a long-term commitment aimed at empowering new disciples to make decisions that will enhance their life in Christ and propel them into the ministry to which God is calling them. Today, I would put this aspect into the metaphor of coaching. A coach begins by teaching the novice how to understand and play the game. As the player's knowledge and skill level increases, the coach pushes the player to develop more skills, to grow in knowledge and experience, and to use that knowledge and experience to be a better player. Eventually the coach gets out of the way and encourages the players from the sidelines. The coach still helps with the game plan or the next play, but the coach is on the sidelines. The goal is to make the player good enough to be a coach to others who are learning the game. We used this same process in helping our pastors understand the process of disciple making.

LEADERSHIP TIP

God is not concerned about our ability or inability.
God is always concerned about our availability.

Fifth Session: Servanthood—Intercessory Prayer

Jesus said, "Whoever wishes to be great among you must be your servant" (Matt. 20:27). We defined servanthood as "laying down our lives for Jesus Christ so that others might find life in Jesus Christ." One way to maintain this servant attitude is to ground yourself in prayer. In this session, we covered issues that dealt with our personal prayer life as well as listening to God and praying for other people. We also explored corporate prayer, the ineffectiveness of spectator prayer, and the need for people to learn intercessory prayer skills such as "praying through" or persevering prayer.[9]

Sixth Session: Visitation Ministries on Their Turf

In this session, we explored the basics of visiting people on their turf, at their homes and businesses. Whether visiting the people in the small group or those who attended Sunday morning worship, there are benefits to making visits to homes by trained pastors. What do you do (and not do) when you make these visits? How can we use the "home visit" to help people encounter the real presence of Jesus? How can we build trust with visitors. Listening skills are crucial in this ministry. Through role-playing, we explored many possibilities and talked in depth about referral procedures when encountering people who need to be seen by doctors, psychologists, or other medical professionals.

Seventh Session: Visitation Ministries at Hospitals and Other Institutions

When visiting in a hospital, how can you maximize the effect of the visit? Practical considerations in hospital and institutional visitations are:

1. the type of illness or crisis the person is facing,
2. the condition of the family or people gathered,
3. what to say and what not to say,
4. how to pray,
5. identifying yourself to the nurses on the floor if you are visiting at off hours,
6. listening skills,
7. the use of the Bible, and
8. making appropriate reports to the church office and, if necessary, to the lead or senior pastor.

We also included a brief overview of visiting in prisons, homeless shelters, and psychiatric facilities.

Eighth Session: Growth Group Leadership

This session focused on the rationale and design of growth groups and the characteristics necessary to be an effective group leader. This session included the design and purpose of growth groups and some characteristics of growth groups. We used material from Bill Easum,[10] Ralph Neighbour Jr.,[11] and Dale Galloway[12] to train people to begin, supervise, and grow these small groups.

Ninth Session: Shepherding Growth Groups

In growth groups, pastors were given the responsibility to teach the group, helping each person find and use his or her spiritual gifts and equipping each member to reach out to those who do not know of God's love in Jesus. Small groups are the most fertile ground for disciple making and for helping believers grow in knowledge of God's love and in love for each other. In these small gatherings, believers are given the opportunity to discover and use their spiritual gifts.

In this session, we covered issues that develop in small groups, such as birthing new groups, dealing with special needs and problem individuals, and how to keep the group on track.

Tenth Session: Knowing Your Limits—Being a Part of the Team

The goal of training these pastors is to share the joy of ministry. When trained properly, these pastors will accomplish far more than any number of paid staff while at the same time decrease the pastor's and staff's workload. The goal is to not burn anyone out; so the last session focused on recognizing your limits, keeping your priorities right, doing effective self-care, and staying part of the team. We identified some of the signs of overload. How can you recognize the signs you are burning out? Why is it so important to stay part of a team to which you are accountable and responsible? What is being a lone ranger really about?

In this session, we stressed the importance of permission giving regarding spiritual gifts. That is, once a person discovers his or her gifts and is trained to use them effectively, we must free that person to use the gifts without having to gain the permission of every person on the trustees or other controlling boards. Yes, there is accountability; that is why you must stay a part of the team and meet with each other at least once a month. But there should not be endless hoops we have to jump through to do the ministry to which God is calling us. As long as the ministry accomplishes the mission of the congregation with its vision and within its values, no one should have to ask permission to attempt ministry.

Results

The True Pastor's Course resulted in a group of people who then had the skills, knowledge, and permission to be all God was calling them to be. These people were given an opportunity to use their gifts in direct ministry, under the supervision of a coach. This meant that instead of me doing the job of ten people, I had fifteen people doing the job of fifteen people: visiting, teaching, leading, and caring in ways one person could never achieve. What a great relief for me to be free to do the ministry God was calling me to without thinking that I was the only one rowing the boat.

The people who took the course went back to their congregations fired up for their ministry. Some of those people actually were able to use their gifts. One woman had the gift of teaching. In her church, she developed a course on Intercessory prayer and taught the course to the leadership of that congregation. A part of that course was putting love in action. Shortly after teaching the course, she suffered a heart attack, and her heart stopped. After paramedics revived her, they flew her in a helicopter to the local hospital. She remained in a serious condition for weeks. Her congregation came together, prayed for her, and stayed at the hospital while she was in a semicomatose condition. As she recovered, they kept the vigil up, praying for her and caring for her family. They prepared a great reception for her when she, against all expectations, fully recovered and returned to worship and to using her gifts of teaching.

The purpose of the course was to empower and train people to use the gifts God has graciously given us to help the congregation fulfill its mission, *that all might know Jesus.* We met the purpose, and these newly empowered people began reaching more and more people for Jesus Christ.

Joyce

Joyce was a key player at East Canton. While operating her own business, she also gave herself to ministry. She caught the vision *that all might know Jesus.* She shared the passion to give each person permission for his or her own ministry. She labored over so many areas in the church, shepherding a growth group and living a servant life.

One of the people in Joyce's small group, Nancy, was another key player in the church. A year after the new building was dedicated, Nancy was diagnosed with cancer. As her growth group leader and friend, Joyce was in constant ministry with and to Nancy and her family. Joyce was at Nancy's side, praying for her, caring for her, encouraging her, as well as caring for Nancy's family. Joyce was at Nancy's side as Nancy died. It was a painful, agonizing ordeal for Nancy's family. Without Joyce's involvement, it would have been much worse. Joyce brought the presence of God into Nancy's home: holding her, bathing her, caring for her and her husband and sons. Joyce was Nancy's pastor, giving her heart to a sister in Christ, laying down her life as servant, telling relatives the good news of God's love, and learning with Nancy the lesson that God is with us through the valley of death.

Joyce continued serving God, running the small group and becoming much of the fuel and energy behind many of the new ideas and projects East Canton would attempt in the next years. She also became the target of many of those who resisted change and who wanted control. Joyce's involvement in ministry was a demonstration that each one of us has a ministry and that the pastor should not do it all. Joyce did not think of herself as pastor, but she was a terrific pastor to so many. I learned much from her.

At East Canton, there were a number of people who were eager to do ministry. Of all of them, Joyce was the most dedicated, the most consistent, the most encouraging, and even the most challenging as she often rebuked me in those times when I was angry, impatient, and ready for a good fight. Her constant words to me were "inch by inch, it's a cinch; yard by yard, the going's hard." Her prayers, dedication to Jesus, servant's life, and love for the congregation were inspirational. She never went to seminary, but she is called and gifted. She, like so many others, was a true pastor at East Canton.

As I said earlier, many are called—far more than the few who have jumped through the hoops to "professional ordination." I have been blessed to know many great pastors. Only a few of them were professional, but many of them were called by God, gifted by the Holy Spirit, and waiting for the empowering permission by the official leadership of the congregation.

Well, now the cat is out of the bag. Amateurs—serious, deep, powerful volunteers in ministry—are the army I want to recruit, train, equip, and send forth into the cities and towns around the world. I do not believe this will put "professional" pastors out of a job. There are many true pastors for us to identify, train, and send out. It would be a viable life's work to accomplish that in your congregation. Think of how many people could be reached if we could recruit this army—gifted by God, powered by the Spirit, and alive for Jesus—and send it out. Can you envision it?

If these true pastors are the leaders of the church, how does that change your role? You might want to reread previous chapters in this new light. Just a thought.

TEN

The Drive for Quality and the Difference Excellence Can Make

Mediocrity seems to dominate life in America today. We will tolerate poor shows, lackluster performances, and halfhearted efforts. The church, once known as the center of excellence with a drive for perfection, is presently at home with half commitments and offerings that are often less than our best.

This condition seems to be a part of the degeneration of the culture as a whole, for I see this acceptance of mediocrity in all but a handful of congregations. Many churches I have worked with are content with mediocrity in every aspect of congregational life. The tendency "not to expect the best" allows anyone to be an expert and to offer his or her opinion on any matter. Consider these cases:

- The sound of the choir, which often painfully afflicts our ears with overblown basses or squeaky sopranos, is the rule in many congregations. The notion that people "audition" for the choir or band is almost unheard of. Why would we allow a person who cannot sing or play to be leading worship and causing such pain?
- The "guest soloist" tried his best to find a note but could not carry it very far.

- The "guest preacher" could pound the pulpit with the fire of Elijah but misquoted every verse and preached twenty-seven poor sermons in the forty-five minutes he spoke (yes, I told him 20 minutes, but they did not teach him that at his church).

Churches accept poor performances so often that no one expects much above mediocrity in many congregations today.

When you live in a rural community, you often learn to "get by" with many things. You learn to fix machines with coat hangers or binder twine (the stringlike material you used to bind hay bales together). When the washer breaks, you learn that panty hose tied tightly around the drive wheel will last long enough to empty the water. Most important you learn that duct tape will hold almost everything together. You get by. You make do.

In a nearby town, I witnessed acceptance of mediocrity during the spring concert of the "vocal club." Most of the singers were young and enthusiastic. They sang with their hearts and offered some quality music. One young lady stood at her appointed time, went forward, and asked for the lead note. Her accompanist gave the starting note. The young lady attempted to sing the first note, hit it flat, and stopped. She *would not* try again. She told her accompanist, "I'm not trying again." What followed surprised me—the crowd applauded. That's right, they applauded. They applauded just as loud as they did for the young lady before her who tried very hard to sing well. This scene was repeated twice. Like the soldier in *The Red Badge of Courage*, she received an honor that was not due her.

In our congregations, all too often we expect applause for just showing up. We frequently do not give our best to the causes we claim to love. We frequently find ourselves bemoaning the process, the gatherings, the meetings, and even the new people. We disgrace our call by living lives that tolerate mediocrity. In the world of the hard-working, laboring families around us, there often was not enough energy or money to do everything well. Expenses were up; incomes were down. Survival was the goal. Maybe next year prices would be better. Getting by becomes the operational guide to life.

Good enough was not ever good enough. If we could not give our best, we would be selling ourselves short and undermining our mission. Only by pushing to be our best would we break out of the depressive and deadly cycle of mediocrity and disappointment.

Perhaps you think I have changed personalities. How dare I speak of God's grace for us in one breath and then push the church to be the best it can be? How can I accept wretchedness in the lives of those who do not know Christ, even saying we need to love and like pre-Christian people, but make it sound as if to be a part of the church you must be perfect? For me it is simple.

When I talk about God's grace, I believe God's grace is high and wide and deep and full, beyond our ability to fathom. We will never exhaust God's love for us. No matter what we do, what we did, where we go, where we went, God loves us. God's love for us is captured in the parable of the searching father in Luke 15. Here, the father is watching for the lost child, ready to embrace the child as soon as he leaves the pigpen and goes home.

My experience of God's grace is centered in the living presence of God in Jesus Christ. I remember leaving the pigpen and taking a journey to meet a God who would accept me, even knowing about all the selfish, mean, cruel, self-seeking garbage in my life. I know what it means to leave the pigpen and find a party. This experience transformed my life. That experience propelled me to embrace all God has for me, even when it has been painful. This experience of God's grace continues to push me to want to know more, learn more, grow more, and share more, that others might know this same wonderful, life-giving presence. I have also learned that when others know the life-giving presence of Jesus, they get to come to the party, too, and in turn get a fire in their souls about knowing more, learning more, growing more, sharing more, and being more than they ever thought possible.

So why a chapter on quality in a book about *small-church turnaround?*

First, this story is about a congregation who gave consistent, quality care to families (many families) and individuals and who did it when it was not easy or convenient and even to those who were "outsiders." This congregation spent money, effort, and—most precious of all—time on people who were often low in hope and desperate. This congregation reached out to others the community said were lost causes. It is wonderful that God still specializes in lost causes!

What this congregation did was equip, empower, and send many people doing many different ministries to surround people with God's care in human form. This congregation was not willing to allow mediocrity to determine what would or would not get accomplished. People regularly gave time, prayed, visited, gave rides, provided resources, and watched children, and as a result, lives were changed.

Second, this story tells about the real motivation for quality in ministry. The motivation to be our best is the love of God found in a relationship with Jesus Christ that picks lives up from the pigpen and deposits us on the Way, transforming the pain and agony of the past into hope for the future and an abundance of life in the soul. Because of this transformation, lives in every part of the county are being touched continuously for God.

Remember Duane and his family? Duane, his wife, and his children have become the voice of God, heard by people who "knew them when" and who cannot argue with the effects of transformation in their lives. His children are leaders in the high school Christian fellowship and are known miles away as part of the spiritual leaders in the youth community. His children lead worship at a contemporary service that focuses on this transformational power. They have seen what happened to their dad. They will never forget. They will never be ashamed of the name that brought their dad back from the pigpen and into the new life in Christ. And they want that life in themselves as well. They know the pressures, the pains, the agony. They know the results of pigpen living. And they know the transforming power of Jesus Christ in a life turned around.

Third, it really does take a congregation committed to Christ and committed to quality in its ministry to make these kinds of differences in people's lives. One or two people would not have the time, energy, or gifts to bring this about. This kind of congregation, grasped by the vision of transformation, is able to offer real life to many. It requires a team to make a difference. So many pastors are burned out because they are alone in attempting to do ministry. How many pastors are no longer serving because the need was so great and those who answered the call were so few? The combination caused them to give more of themselves than they could without burning out.

Fourth, the ministry needs of our world demand quality in everything we attempt. I do not look for perfection in these areas, but I always push for more time, more dedication, and more effort from myself and from God's people. I push for more because the people around us need real demonstrations of God's love done with excellence. So much more was given for me and for you, and when I live from that reservoir, I have so much more to give and seem to get so much more back than I ever thought of giving. Whether it is in our worship, in our growth groups, through our choirs or bands, with our true pastors, or in our care or counseling efforts—no matter what ministry we have it is much more effective when we rely on God's reserves. Ask God for bigger visions, bigger dreams, more energy. Push to be the best you can be. Push others to be the best they can be.

Fifth, and maybe most important, this story can be your story. Your congregation can be transformed as well. This is not a "once-in-a-lifetime event." God is in the business of bringing dead things to life. God is a specialist at taking broken things (lives and congregations) and mending them for the purpose of changing the world.

Quality Ministry Calls for Critical Evaluation

At East Canton, we constantly strove to do everything we did better. We evaluated everything we did, from greeting visitors in the parking lot to baking bread for these visitors' Sunday lunch. We evaluated our choice of songs and the content of the message. We evaluated the appearance of the building and the cleanliness of the rest rooms and nursery. We always tried to show how much we loved God by being our best.

We did not always meet our standards, but we never failed, because the only way to fail in Christ is to quit. We never quit. Every project, mission, or congregational event had an evaluation process attached to it. After every event, we wanted details of the event, changes the leaders would make if and when attempting that again, and a clear understanding of how this project met or did not meet the mission of the congregation.

In 1996, I took a group of leaders to a Community Church of Joy event in Philadelphia. Some of that group went to Walt Kallestad's seminar "Total Quality Ministry."[1] They came back excited with new ideas to improve our evaluation process. One woman said, "That was great but sad, too.

We were the only other congregation in that seminar that regularly evaluates what we do. Why don't others do this?"

I would ask you to evaluate everything your church does. What would it look like if it were better? How can you improve? Can you give the people in those ministries the permission to make changes that will improve the ministry without their having to jump through hoops? The U.S. Army had this slogan, "Be All That You Can Be." I liked that slogan! What if you were being "all you can be" in the ministry God is giving you? What if you could be more? What if you did not settle for what they tell you and you started right now to believe you could be more? What if you gave up on the idea that you should get rewarded for just showing up? What if you believed you could:

- leave the pigpen,
- be more than a failure,
- be more than just "good enough,"
- be more than a dying church,
- be more than a fair pastor,
- be more than a barely faithful worship attendee,
- become more than an elite skeptic,
- have more than a small church,
- become more than a large church,
- be more than a good singer,
- be more than a pew warmer, and
- be more than just a child or an adult—retired or working.

What if it were true that God was "able to do immeasurably more than all we ask or imagine" (Eph. 3:20 NIV)? What if that were true for your life, your congregation?

ELEVEN

If It Could Happen Here, It Could Happen Where You Are!

By 1993, East Canton was on a roll. We continued to grow. More people were praying than ever before. We knew why we were here. We were going to reach our mission, *that all might know Jesus.* We were committed to going forward. We were in the process of renovation and building. The responsibilities of ministry were in the hands of gifted laypeople. Our worship was upbeat, warm, expectant, filled with a sense of God with us. More people were in worship than ever before. It was fun to be there. Over fourteen small groups were meeting each week, involving over 130 people. New groups were forming, and new leaders were developing. Membership was a commitment to Christ and to the mission of the East Canton congregation. Membership was drawing some great people into leadership. Our committee-less structure gave us more opportunity to be involved in direct ministry. Ideas for ministry began to explode. By December 1993, the new building was finished in time for the Christmas Eve service. In January 1994, we held a dedication service, and—you guessed it—we did not build large enough. We were packed with over three hundred in worship that Sunday afternoon.

By 1995, I was able to take a three-month educational sabbatical from the responsibilities of the church and counseling clinic. In the three months I was away, they did not miss me. The leaders of the congregation were already doing the majority of the ministry, and in this three-month period, they were able to continue with the ministry without missing a beat. In fact, worship attendance went up in those three months! I spent those three months visiting dynamic congregations all across the United States. Most helpful in this time was my week at the Community Church of Joy. Two of the church's staff, Tim Wright and Ginny Thomas, were extremely helpful to me. When I returned to East Canton, I was assured we were on the right track, and I had a larger vision than before. And now with three months of rest, I had the energy for the work it would require to develop East Canton into a "teaching church." I saw the potential of taking the lessons we learned at East Canton and inviting people to come and "experience" a weekend with us.

That weekend eventually became the seminar "Preparing God's People," which is the basis of this work. We hosted many congregations at East Canton for a weekend event that focused on each lever we used to turn this church around. We also took "the show on the road," sending teams to many congregations to help them develop growth groups and volunteer-led ministries.

We had so many plans and so many ministry ideas ready to launch that we were a bit shocked to learn that I was to be moved, that is, to have my appointment changed in 1996. This was a wake-up call, reminding me of the transitory nature of so much of life. It was a God thing, too. It got me focused on the priority of East Canton becoming a station church, having the oversight of a full-time pastor to propel them to greater effectiveness in ministry, and using their resources for ministry in the area. After a long discussion with the bishop, I was able to stay at East Canton to make the dream of becoming a station congregation a reality. After six more months, East Canton (and Windfall) was given permission to be a station church. Effective July 1997, East Canton would be free to be all that she could envision and dream.

By this time, it was also clear that I would be moving out of full-time parish ministry. The counseling clinic was expanding, as was my relationship with what is now Easum, Bandy & Associates. I had the opportunity to begin a new era for the clinic with a new office in a larger city.

In late June of 1997, my family and I packed our belongings and moved from East Canton. It was a painful time. The grief was intense for much of that summer and fall.

At the end of the eleven years of ministry with those people, we all had grown. This experience changed almost everything we thought about ministry, and we discovered that God really was able to do "immeasurably more than all we ask or imagine." I continue to carry these lessons with me. I am so grateful for all those years taught me. The lessons continue to serve me well. It is my hope that these lessons will help you too.

Size is not the issue. Any church can turn around. As Bill Easum said in the *NetResults* article, "If it can happen here, it can happen anywhere."[1] What if that were true for you and your congregation? What if your church could turn around, too?

It has now been five years since I left East Canton. Some of the people who were there have moved away. Worship attendance at two services is under one hundred people. The appointment that followed me was difficult for almost everyone. Because of the sudden death of that pastor, another pastor was recently appointed, and there is a new hope in many. For some, the hope will center in whether or not they can teach him "pastor fetch." For some, the hope will be whether or not the congregation will go forward or retreat into the dark and dank world of the dying church movement.

I do not go back to East Canton. I do not stick my nose there. Obviously after eleven years of ministry in that location, some people still call to talk, cry, pray, or remember. I attempt to push them to dream forward. We cannot live in the past. I am convinced that the right now is so important that I do not like to think about what was. I still wonder what can be.

I do not hold out much hope for visionless, mission-less congregations. If you do not know where you are going, any road will get you there. "Without a vision the people go to another parish."[2] Congregations that have no passion are like marriages that no longer have a spark. I do not care what the reason is, but without the spark, the car won't run, the marriage won't last, and the church won't function in any way that looks like a church. And frankly, we do not need more country clubs.

I do think that God is able to do "immeasurably more than all we ask or imagine" (Eph. 3:20 NIV). I have watched it, wondered at it, seen it, tasted it, and know it is true. What a wonderful journey it was at East Canton during those years.

It is my hope that you have caught a picture of what your congregation can be. It is my hope that you have an idea, "a vague beginning or stirring of ideas,"[3] that will propel you and your congregation into greater ministry and effectiveness. Remember, there is always someone with a bucket of water ready to put out any fire burning in your soul. Do not let the fire die. Fan the flame, let it burn, making you and your congregation *a light for those in darkness and safety for those in storms, that all might know Jesus.*

In closing, I want to remind you that this was from the beginning the Lord's work. The wonderful turnaround experience at East Canton was because God is eager to use people to win people, to love people, and to save people. God is eager to have the world know of his love. God is able to do so much more! Begin to apply each lever to your situation. Take one at a time. The order that worked best for us is presented here; you may find another order works for you. I encourage you to start with prayer (Lever 1). Ask God to help you. Ask God what you need to make a turn-around possible in your congregation. Ask God to help you adjust to the changes you will experience.

The point of this project is that you and your congregation might experience the wonder and transformational power of God to turn lives and congregations around. If it could happen here, I know it could happen where you are. If it could happen here, it could happen anywhere!

Notes

Introduction

1. William M. Easum, *The Complete Ministry Audit: How to Measure Twenty Principles for Growth* (Nashville: Abingdon Press, 1996), 112.

2. William M. Easum, "If It Can Work Here, It Can Work Anywhere," *NetResults* (January 1997): 13.

3. Tex Sample, *Hard Living People and Mainstream Christians* (Nashville: Abingdon Press, 1993).

4. Many of these farmers owned between two hundred and twelve hundred acres of land, large barns, numerous tractors, and farm machinery. Cash was scarce. Their money was tied up in land, cattle, and machines. One family was paid only $100 per month. Yes, the farm paid all the other bills, but that still was not much money for a family of five.

5. Dale E. Galloway, *20/20 Vision: How to Create a Successful Church with Lay Pastors and Cell Groups* (Portland, Ore.: Scott Publishing Company, 1986), 9.

1. Then and Now

1. Loren B. Mead, *The Once and Future Church: Reinventing the Congregation for a New Mission Frontier* (Washington, D.C.: Alban Institute, 1991), 8-29.

2. George Barna, *The Barna Report* (May/June 1997): 2.

3. Bob Dylan, "The Times They Are a-Changin'," recorded by Peter, Paul, and Mary. *In Concert*, Warner Brothers Records, 1963.

4. Leonard Sweet, *AquaChurch* (Loveland, Colo.: Group Publishing, 1999), 125.

5. Bill Hybels at Willow Creek, Wayne Cordero at New Hope Community Church.

6. Len Wilson, *The Wired Church: Making Media Ministry* (Nashville: Abingdon Press, 1999).

2. "Light for Those in Darkness, Safety for Those in Storms"

1. Terry Teykl, *Your Pastor: Preyed On or Prayed For* (Anderson, Ind.: Bristol Books, 1994). Check the Internet site www.renewalministries. com for more information.

2. Henry T. Blackaby and Claude V. King, *Experiencing God: How to Live the Full Adventure of Knowing and Doing the Will of God* (Nashville: Broadman & Holman Publishers, 1994).

3. I dislike the artificial distinction of clergy and laity. I have struggled with other terms, like "Christian amateurs" or "Volunteers." I like the Greek *laos*, meaning the people of God. All believers are *laos*, including the pastor. In this book, I will use the term laity but will consistently argue against a "two-class" system of ordained and nonordained. We all are called, gifted, and ordained by God.

4. We attempted a second service one summer with only moderate results. It was sabotaged by its early time, by the lack of child care, and by the second worship service beginning immediately after the first service with Sunday school occurring two hours after the start of the first service.

3. The End of "Pastor Fetch" and the Beginning of "People Go"

1. Bill Easum, *How to Reach Baby Boomers* (Nashville: Abingdon Press, 1991), 29.

2. Thomas G. Bandy, *Kicking Habits: Welcome Relief for Addicted Churches* (Nashville: Abingdon Press, 1997), 27-31.

3. While there exists no known tribe of this classification, the offspring of these people are quite common in the church today.

4. Bob Mumford, *Growing Oaks of Righteousness,* audiocassette (1996).

5. William Easum, *Easum Bandy 2000 Tour* (Philadelphia, March 14, 2000).

4. Lever 1: Prayer

1. Francis A. Schaeffer, *He Is There and He Is Not Silent* (Wheaton, Ill.: Tyndale House Publishers, 1972).

2. Terry Teykl, *Your Pastor: Preyed On or Prayed For* (Anderson, Ind.: Bristol Books, 1994).

5. Lever 2: Discerning a Clear Mission

1. Percept Group, Inc. 800-442-6277 or call Stanley Menking at 570-646-0973 or E-mail smenking@epix.net. The cost is $310.00.

2. Walt Kallestad, Community Church of Joy Conference (Philadelphia, August 1994).

3. *The Book of Discipline of The United Methodist Church* (Nashville: The United Methodist Publishing House, 1996). In recent years the *Discipline* has been reorganized to provide opportunity for new structures that facilitate ministry.

6. Lever 3: Indigenous Worship

1. Indigenous, *adjective*, 1. Originating and growing or living in an area or environment; 2. Intrinsic, innate (*American Heritage Dictionary*, third ed.).

2. See Tim Wright, *A Community of Joy: How to Create Contemporary Worship* (Nashville: Abingdon Press, 1989), for great series topics.

3. Lyle E. Schaller, *The InterVentionist* (Nashville: Abingdon Press, 1997). See his discussion on European versus American styles and the implications for worship, polity, and praxis.

7. Lever 4: Growth Groups

1. Growth Groups is an attempt to differentiate between 1960s small, informal study groups, 1980s highly structured and highly managed curriculum-based groups, and what occurred at East Canton. These in-home groups were the primary vehicle for care, adult spiritual formation, education, and outreach. At East Canton in 1989, we called these groups "small groups," but we were clear on the distinctions between the past and what we were attempting to accomplish.

2. Dale E. Galloway, *20/20 Vision: How to Create a Successful Church with Lay Pastors and Cell Groups* (Portland, Ore.: Scott Publishing Company, 1986).

3. Mark belonged to the other church on the charge, Windfall. But Mark was a part of both congregations, leading many joint services, codirecting the East Canton building project, and involvement with all the training and disciple-making projects at East Canton.

4. Ralph W. Neighbour, Jr., *Where Do We Go from Here? A Guidebook for Cell Group Churches* (Houston: Touch Publications, 1990).

8. Lever 5: Membership That Means Something

1. For people who are really into counting numbers, worship attendance is the real number to count.

2. Bill Easum, *Leadership on the OtherSide: No Rules, Just Clues* (Nashville: Abingdon Press, 2000), 88-90.

3. Walt Kallestad, "Evangelism Event," Community Church of Joy (Philadelphia, August 1996).

4. The Envisioning Team was the dreaming team at East Canton Church. Once a month, the Team met to dream "impossible" dreams, which would enable us to fulfill the mission *that all might know Jesus* by being light for those in darkness and safety for those in storms.

9. Lever 6: Lay Pastoring

1. Thomas G. Bandy, *Kicking Habits: Welcome Relief for Addicted Churches* (Nashville: Abingdon Press, 1997).

2. I originally used the title "Lay Pastor" because many traditional church people would understand the word "lay" to mean "nonprofessional and nonordained." To steer clear of that artificial separation between "clergy and lay," I have chosen to simply call these people "true pastors" as defined in Ephesians 4:11-15.

3. Originally called "Lay Pastor's Course."

4. Loren B. Mead, *The Once and Future Church* (Washington, D.C.: Alban Institute, 1991).

5. William Easum, *Church Growth Handbook* (Nashville: Abingdon Press, 1990).

6. Earl Holmes, "God Centered Listening," address given at Messiah College, *Faith at Work Conference* (Grantham, Pa., 1972).

7. Lester Luborsky, *Principles of Psychoanalytic Psychotherapy* (New York: Basic Books, 1984).

8. Bill Bright, *Witnessing Without Fear* (Nashville: Thomas Nelson Publishers, 1993), 82-83.

9. Dwight L. Moody, *Persevering Prayer* (Chicago: Moody Press, 1939),

10. William Easum, *L.I.F.E. Workbook: Living in Faith Everyday* (Port Aransas: William Easum, 1992).

11. Ralph W. Neighbour, Jr. *Where Do We Go from Here? A Guidebook for the Cell Group Church* (Houston: Touch Publications, 1990).

12. Dale E. Galloway, *20/20 Vision: How to Create a Successful Church with Lay Pastors and Cell Groups* (Portland, Ore.: Scott Publishing Company, 1986).

10. The Drive for Quality and the Difference Excellence Can Make

1. Walt Kallestad and Steven L. Schey, *Total Quality Ministry* (Minneapolis: Augsburg Press, 1994).

11. If It Could Happen Here, It Could Happen Where You Are!

1. William Easum, "If It Can Work Here, It Can Work Anywhere," *NetResults* (January 1997): 13.

2. Walt Kallestad, Live presentation (Philadelphia, 1996).

3. Dale E. Galloway, *20/20 Vision: How to Create a Successful Church with Lay Pastors and Cell Groups* (Portland, Ore.: Scott Publishing Company, 1986).

Bibliography

Bandy, Thomas G. *Christian Chaos: Revolutionizing the Congregation.* Nashville: Abingdon Press, 1999.

_____. *Coaching Change: Breaking Down Resistance, Building Up Hope.* Nashville: Abingdon Press, 2000.

_____. *Kicking Habits: Welcome Relief for Addicted Churches.* Nashville: Abingdon Press, 1997.

_____. *Moving Off the Map: A Field Guide to Changing the Congregation.* Nashville: Abingdon Press, 1998.

Barna, George. *User Friendly Churches.* Ventura, Calif.: Regal Books, 1991.

_____. *The Barna Report.* Ventura, Calif.: The Barna Research Group. Published quarterly through fall of 1999.

Barnett, Tommy. *Portraits of Vision.* Nashville: Thomas Nelson Publishers, 1990.

Benedict, Daniel T., and Craig Kennet Miller. *Contemporary Worship for the 21st Century: Worship or Evangelism?* Nashville: Discipleship Resources, 1994.

Bible, Life Application, New International Version, Wheaton, Ill.: Tyndal House Publishers, Inc. 1991.

Blackaby, Henry T., and Claude V. King. *Experiencing God: How to Live the Full Adventure of Knowing and Doing the Will of God.* Nashville: Broadman and Holman Publishers, 1994.

Bright, Bill. *Witnessing Without Fear.* Nashville: Thomas Nelson Publishers, 1993.

Dobson, Ed. *Starting a Seeker Sensitive Service: How Traditional Churches Can Reach the Unchurched.* Grand Rapids, Mich.: Zondervan Publishing House, 1993.

Dylan, Bob. "The Times They Are a-Changin'." As recorded by Peter, Paul, and Mary, *In Concert*, Warner Brothers Records, 1963.

Easum, William M. *Church Growth Handbook: Includes Complete Ministry Audit.* Nashville: Abingdon Press, 1990.

_____. *The Complete Ministry Audit: How to Measure Twenty Principles for Growth.* Nashville: Abingdon Press, 1996.

_____. *Dancing with Dinosaurs: Ministry in a Hostile and Hurting World.* Nashville: Abingdon Press, 1993.

_____. "If It Can Work Here, It Can Work Anywhere." *NetResults* (January 1997), pp. 13-15.

_____. *Leadership on the OtherSide: No Rules, Just Clues.* Nashville: Abingdon Press, 2000.

_____. *Living in Faith Everyday—A Workbook for L.I.F.E. Groups.* Port Arnasas, Tex.: William Easum, 1992.

_____. *Sacred Cows Make Gourmet Burgers: Ministry Anytime, Anywhere by Anybody.* Nashville: Abingdon Press, 1995.

Easum, William M., and Thomas G. Bandy. *Growing Spiritual Redwoods.* Nashville: Abingdon Press, 1997.

Fox, H. Eddie and George E. Morris. *Faith Sharing: Dynamic Christian Witnessing by Invitation.* Nashville: Discipleship Resources, 1986.

Friedman, Edwin H. *Generation to Generation: Family Process in Church and Synagogue.* New York: Guilford Press, 1985.

Galloway, Dale. *20/20 Vision: How to Create a Successful Church with Lay Pastors and Cell Groups.* Portland, Ore.: Scott Publishing Company, 1986.

Hawkins, Thomas R. *Building God's People: A Workbook for Empowering Servant Leaders.* Nashville: Discipleship Resources, 1990.

Hunt, Gladys. *You Can Start a Bible Study Group: Making Friends, Changing Lives.* Wheaton, Ill.: Harold Shaw Publishers, 1989.

Hunter, George G., III. *Church for the Unchurched.* Nashville: Abingdon Press, 1996.

_____. *How to Reach Secular People.* Nashville: Abingdon Press, 1992.

Hybels, Lynne, and Bill Hybels. *Rediscovering Church: The Story and Vision of Willow Creek Community Church.* Grand Rapids, Mich.: Zondervan Publishing House, 1995.

Kallestad, Walt. *Entertainment Evangelism: Taking the Church Public.* Nashville: Abingdon Press, 1996.

Kallestad, Walt, and Steven L. Schey. *Total Quality Ministry.* Minneapolis: Augsburg Press, 1994.

Lewis, Phillip V. *Transformational Leadership: A New Model for Total Church Involvement.* Nashville: Broadman & Holman Publishers, 1996.

Luborsky, Lester. *Principles of Psychoanalytic Psychotherapy: A Manual for Supportive-Expressive Treatment.* New York: Basic Books, 1984.

MacArthur, John, Jr. *Rediscovering Pastoral Ministry: Shaping Contemporary Ministry with Biblical Mandate.* Dallas: Word Publishing, 1995.

Mead, Loren B. *The Once and Future Church: Reinventing the Congregation for a New Mission Frontier.* Washington, D.C.: Alban Institute, 1991.

_____. *Transforming Congregations for the Future.* Bethesda, Md.: Alban Institute, 1994.

Neighbour, Ralph W., Jr. *Where Do We Go from Here? A Guidebook for Cell Group Churches.* Houston: Touch Publications, 1990.

Oden, Thomas C. *Requiem: A Lament in Three Movements.* Nashville: Abingdon Press, 1995.

Rutz, James H. *The Open Church: How to Bring Back the Exciting Life of the First Century Church.* Auburn, Me.: SeedSowers Press, 1992.

Sample, Tex. *Hard Living People and Mainstream Christians.* Nashville: Abingdon Press, 1993.

_____. *The Spectacle of Worship in a Wired World: Electronic Culture and the Gathered People of God.* Nashville: Abingdon Press, 1998.

_____. *White Soul: Country Music, the Church, and Working Americans.* Nashville: Abingdon Press, 1996.

Schaeffer, Francis A. *He Is There and He Is Not Silent.* Wheaton, Ill.: Tyndale House Publishers, 1972.

Schaller, Lyle E. *The InterVentionist.* Nashville: Abingdon Press, 1997.

_____. *The New Reformation: Tomorrow Arrived Yesterday.* Nashville: Abingdon Press, 1995.

_____. *The Very Large Church.* Nashville: Abingdon Press, 2000.

Scott, Dan. *The Emerging American Church.* Anderson, Ind.: Bristol Books, 1993.

Slaughter, Michael. *Out on the Edge: A Wake-up Call for Church Leaders on the Edge of the Media Reformation.* Nashville: Abingdon Press, 1998.

_____. *Spiritual Entrepreneurs: Six Principles for Risking Renewal.* Nashville: Abingdon Press, 1995.

Sweet, Leonard. *AquaChurch.* Loveland, Colo.: Group Publishing, 1999.

_____. *Soul Tsunami: Sink or Swim in New Millennium Culture.* Grand Rapids, Mich.: Zondervan Publishing, 1999.

Teykl, Terry. *Blueprint for the House of Prayer.* Muncie, Ind.: Prayer Point Press, 1996.

_____. *Your Pastor: Preyed On or Prayed For.* Anderson, Ind.: Bristol Books, 1994.

_____. *Pray the Price.* Muncie, Ind.: Prayer Point Press, 1997.

Warren, Rick. *The Purpose Driven Church: Growth Without Compromising Your Message and Mission.* Grand Rapids, Mich.: Zondervan Publishing House, 1995.

Wills, Dick. *Waking to God's Dream: Spiritual Leadership and Church Renewal.* Nashville: Abingdon Press, 1999.

Wilson, Len. *The Wired Church: Making Media Ministry.* Nashville: Abingdon Press, 1999.

Wright, Tim. *A Community of Joy: How to Create Contemporary Worship.* Nashville: Abingdon Press, 1994.

Wright, Tim, and Jan Wright, ed. *Contemporary Worship: A Sourcebook for Spirited-Traditional, Praise and Seeker Services.* Nashville: Abingdon Press, 1997.